Messages

CW01024417

The Masters about Karma

Dictated to the Messenger Tatyana N. Mickushina

March 2005 – January 2007

Tatyana N. Mickushina

BOOKSURGE

The Masters about Karma

Dictated to the Messenger
Tatyana N. Mickushina

Translated from Russian by
Svetlana Nekrasova

This book contains the messages received by Tatyana N. Mickushina from the Ascended Masters. By now there have been 20 books written and published in the Russian language.

The messages are constantly being translated into different languages by people all around the world. At present there are 19 languages that the messages are being translated into.

This particular book covers the subject of Karma. The Masters explain in detail all the nuances of the Law of Cause and Effect and how we face this law in our everyday life.

Websites:
http://sirius-eng.net (English version)
http://sirius-ru.net (Russian version)

ISBN: 1-4392-5511-3
ISBN-13: 9781439255117

Visit **www.booksurge.com**
to order additional copies.

Table of Contents

From the author

I was born and I live in Russia in the south of western Siberia in the city of Omsk. During all my life I have been praying and asking God to grant me an opportunity to work for Him.

In 2004 I was granted a Messenger's Mantle of the Great White Brotherhood and received an opportunity to bring the Words of the Masters to people. During the years 2005-2009 at certain periods of time I have been receiving messages of the Ascended Masters in a special way.

I am very happy that with the help of many people the messages I received have been translated into English and the English-speaking readers can become familiar with them.

The only thing the Ascended Masters want is to spread their Teaching throughout the world. The Masters give their messages with the feeling of great Love.

Love has no limits. There are no boundaries between the hearts of people living in different countries, there are no boundaries between the worlds. The boundaries exist only in the consciousness of people.

The Masters appeal through me to every human living on planet Earth.

From Siberia with Love,

Tatyana Mickushina

Preface

This book contains the selection from the dictations which the Ascended Masters were giving through their messenger Tatyana Mickushina during the period from March 4, 2005 till January 10, 2007.

These dictations pertain to one general topic. The Masters speak about karma. Much of the knowledge given by the Masters about karma reveals the notion of karma in a new perspective.

What is karma? Why should a human get free from karma? How can it be done fastest and as efficiently as possible?

In reality the knowledge of the Law of Karma or the Law of Retribution is the most important knowledge at this time. And the more people can familiarise themselves with the notion of karma and are guided in their lives by the knowledge received, the faster humanity as a whole will be able to get rid of the problems inherent in it at this stage of development.

"Man's memory is very short and, as a rule, it is very difficult for man to follow a direct link between the actions he performs in life and their consequences. But it is exactly this connection that is at the basis of the Law of Karma or so-called Law of Cause and Effect and Retribution."

"Just one of your vibrations of Love and Compassion
is capable of extinguishing the fire of hell where
many souls of this planet are burning now"
Beloved Hilarion, April 10, 2005

"If you scrutinise your life attentively, you may notice that exactly the same problems, connected with your state of mind and your perception of yourself and

the surrounding world, crop up in front of you with enviable periodicity. The spring keeps unwinding, and with each of its circles the same problems return to you with enviable constancy. And again you have to return to the qualities you have not worked out to solve life problems cropping up in front of you each time at a new level.

All this resembles ocean waves lapping against the shore. A wave runs over the shore and then recedes. While moving, a wave embroils stones lying on the shore of the ocean and carries them away. After thousands of years stones become smooth. Any roughness is polished by the ocean. In the very same way God polishes your imperfect qualities day after day, year after year, in accordance with the Law of Cosmic Cycles, until you become smooth and your aura acquires the right oval form, the transparency and the tints that were inherent in your soul primordially before you undertook your embodiment in the physical world. This process of polishing your qualities and transforming them into the Divine ones lasts for many lives.

A wise man understands that it is impossible to pass by the force of the Cosmic Law, but the result to which this Law directs you may be achieved during a shorter period of time, if you do not resist the Law, but help to observe it. In this case you may achieve results during fewer cosmic cycles. All this explains the meaning of the saying that the days of the chosen people will be shortened.

You have an opportunity to shorten the days of your life on Earth only if you speed up the returning of your karma. While an ordinary person will need tens of years to work out his karma, you will be able to do it in a year. You will just transform the distorted

energy faster owing to your own wish and the Divine mercy which enables you to do it."

"The best sermon will be your personal example"
The Goddess of Liberty, April 22, 2005

"If the knowledge of the Law of karma or the Law of retribution were widespread among the people of earth and especially among the youth, it would be possible to prevent many actions of humans committed by them due to their ignorance.

To know the Law of karma is the first step necessary for every individual in order not to sin but to act in life according to the Divine principles.

Therefore the major task for each of you in the near future is to acquaint the more people the better with the Law of karma or retribution. And the best example will be your own. Show your example to your child, your family, your colleagues at work."

"About the opportunity to unburden your karma of the next month and about the letters to the Karmic Board"
Beloved Surya, June 23, 2005

"You are children. You are sitting on the shore of the ocean of the Divine Wisdom trying to perceive this Wisdom with your childish inquisitive mind. Never leave this childish state of your consciousness. Never become adults in the questions of knowing the Divine Truth.

Be like children, and you will manage to reach such heights in your consciousness which were beyond the comprehension of the previous generations."

"Never become adults in the questions of knowing the Divine Truth"
Beloved Surya, March 9, 2005

Never become adults in the questions of knowing the Divine Truth

Beloved Surya, March 9, 2005

I AM Surya and I have come today from the Great Central Sun to give you the word of God through our Messenger. Almost one year ago I had the honour to lay the mantle of God's Messenger on Tatyana's shoulders.

At that time she could not believe that this event was much more real in her life than everything happening around her in the physical plane.

The mantle of the messenger cannot be taken for granted. It must be deserved. And this merit is not obtained just in one embodiment, it can be acquired in the course of many embodiments during which an individual must prove his/her true devotion to God's Will in order to deserve this mantle.

However, past attainments must be confirmed without fail in the current embodiment. Without that it is impossible for a person to be endowed with this mantle. In the end, the right to be endowed with the mantle depends only on the level of your current attainments, regardless of your successful devotion in the past.

That is why we pay special attention to testing the individuals who have already had the mantles of messengers in the past. We have a few constantly embodied individuals who have already had the mantles in the past and who are potentially ready to confirm their mission of a messenger.

Nevertheless, the decision to endow any of the embodied individuals with the mantle is taken at the highest level, on the Great Central Sun.

That is why I ask you to hold in respect the mantle lying on Tatyana's shoulders.

Immediately after the moment of declaration of her messenger status in public any disrespect shown by you towards our messenger automatically brings you karma between you and God and this kind of karma is the most difficult to transmute.

We protect our messengers. It is not you who decides whom we must choose.

In the present conditions on earth our great task is to manifest the interaction between our messengers. As you know, if two of our physically incarnated messengers met and contacted each other in the past, they did not as a rule recognise each other as messengers and were not able to interact. This was determined by their level of consciousness and could not be surmounted until the moment had come for the new stage of the cosmic opportunity to occur.

Beloved Sanat Kumara has told you through this messenger that the time has changed. It has really changed. We enter the stage when two or more of our messengers will be capable of recognising each other and working together.

The difficulty here is in the fact that one and the same truth is interpreted by the minds of embodied people differently, depending on those systems of world outlook which involved their consciousness from the starting moment of their current embodiment.

It is here that the difficulty has always been – to find the things in common and to develop mutual understanding of those seemingly totally different interpretations of God which were expressed by these embodied individuals through their external consciousness.

Nevertheless, when you rise in your consciousness and reach its higher level you see that the things which seemed before to be an absolute contradiction for your external consciousness are in fact just different points of view and different approaches to one and the same Truth.

Believe me, it is not worth overly disputing any interpretation of this or another Truth by your limited consciousness. Your consciousness is so imperfect that it is simply foolish to declare and to affirm your own truth as the only reliable and infallible one. It can be compared with two people in dispute, one of whom affirms that the Earth is floating in the sea on three whales and the other who proves that the Earth is lying on three elephants.

It seems funny for you even to imagine such a dispute now. However, most religious conflicts and wars had analogical reasons as their basis.

You are children. You are sitting on the shore of the ocean of the Divine Wisdom trying to perceive this Wisdom with your childish inquisitive mind. Never leave this childish state of your consciousness. Never become adults in the questions of knowing the Divine Truth.

Be like children, and you will manage to reach such heights in your consciousness which were beyond the comprehension of the previous generations.

I contemplate the Earth with my spiritual vision. And I see this enlarging precipice separating the consciousness of the people who allow the Divine Truth to settle in their hearts from the consciousness of those sticking to their own interpretation of the Truth because this interpretation seems reliable to them due to the fact that it was handed down to them with the faith of their ancestors. There are also people who have come to such a standstill in their evolution that they have even stopped recollecting the very name of God in their daily routine.

We are ready to render all possible assistance to earthly mankind. We are ready to use all the Heaven's might for giving this help. But we cannot help you until you yourselves ask for it.

What prevents you from applying to your Heavenly Father in your heart and sincerely asking Him for help? What prevents you from doing so?

I will tell you what it is. It is your karma that prevents you, the karma between you and God. Therefore, the most important thing for you now is your wish to overcome this karma in your heart.

God can do everything. But why don't you wish to accept His help? You have forgotten your Source. You have forgotten where you have come from.

Do not hurt my messengers who have come to remind you about that. Remember that any manifestation of your disrespect to God's messengers is a manifestation of your disrespect to God Himself. But this is a heavy sin which can be redeemed only by undergoing great suffering.

I am very sorry to see the people suffering on the Earth. With the help of my message I wish most of these sufferers to understand that you yourselves gave rise to your suffering and you are able to get rid of it just by waving a magic wand. You should just accept God into your heart. You should open your hearts to the Divine Truth and start knowing this Truth like children sitting on the ocean's shore.

I leave you alone with your contemplations about God and His messengers in your heart. I ask you to think about an opportunity for each of you to become my messenger. Messenger status is simply a definite momentum of merits on the path of your sincere devotion to the Divine Truth.

Now I want you to open your hearts. You should wish to get rid of one trait, that one trait, which you think most of all prevents you from progressing on the Path.

Do wish sincerely in your heart to get rid of this trait and I will help you in this. And the extent of my aid will be proportional to your faith in God and the Divine Truth.

This is my present which I want to give you today.

I AM Surya and I look forward to meeting those of you who are ready to accept this new opportunity and the new dispensation

We simply took the matches away from the children

Beloved Surya, March 19, 2005

I AM Surya and I have come today from the Great Central Sun to give you the Teaching on karma through this messenger.

You have known the term karma as the energy which accompanies you during your earthly cycle of embodiments. You get Divine energy which is the source of life in the universe. Further, you utilise this energy in accordance with your free will given by God. But your utilisation of this energy does not always correspond to God's Will. In this case this incorrectly qualified energy supplements your karmic load, being deposited in your higher and physical bodies.

Further, the Law of likeness comes into force. This incorrectly qualified energy, constantly accompanying you in life, brings to you such life situations through which you have to live. It makes you learn a lesson and act in such situations not in accordance with your will, but with the Will of God.

As a matter of fact, you are creating your karma constantly when you break the Will of God and act of your own selfish accord. Therefore, your karma is directly proportional to the level of your egoism, to the level of your isolation from God's Law and to the level of your disagreement with God's Law.

Your correct choices, which you make in each situation conditioned by karma, help you work out your karma. Each such choice brings you nearer to God and makes you reject and part with the unreal part you created.

In accordance with the cosmic cycles, you descend into materiality at the beginning of a cycle, create karma and then leave the material world, as if constantly analysing your previous mistakes. Again and again you are placed into the same situations, which demand that you work out your karma. Such a cycle of your leaving materiality has just begun and it will last for many millions of earthly years.

Let us now examine the dispensation, which has been given to you through our previous messengers, that is the violet-flame dispensation. The essence of the karma transmutation with the help of reading the violet-flame decrees was in the following: during the reading of the decrees you were to realise those traits of yours which were not Divine and to transform these negative qualities into positive or Divine ones with the help of additional Divine energy attracted to your physical world.

What has happened since you received this dispensation? You live in a dual world and this means literally that everything in your world can be used in favour of good, as well as in favour of evil.

You can ask how it is possible to use the reading of the violet-flame decrees, intended for the karma transmutation, in favour of evil. It is very simple, and I can explain it to you now straightforwardly, because the violet-flame dispensation has been withdrawn from planet Earth at present. At that moment when you are drawing to yourself the additional flow of Divine energy during your reading of the decrees, you control this flow through your thoughts and feelings. And if at the moment of receiving this additional energy your thoughts and feelings are not of high purity and are far from Divine perfection, the following thing happens: instead of transmutation of the karmic deposit in the electronic belt of your four lower bodies you add to this deposit the energy which was incorrectly qualified by you at the moment of the reading of the violet-flame decrees. Thus, you create new karma instead of working out your old one.

You see that the violet-flame decrees represented a mighty weapon, given to you at this difficult time for your planet. And you see that 90 percent of this violet-flame energy was forming a sediment in your lower bodies at the moment of the reading of the decrees, because at that moment you were thinking not about getting rid of your ego and imperfection, but were speculating about what you could get from God in exchange for your many hours of vigils. What is worse, in your thoughts you permitted condemnation of your brothers. You permitted other negative thoughts and feelings while reading these decrees.

Therefore, the violet-flame dispensation has a selective function at present. It is in force only for those groups and people who have a correct inner motive when starting to read the violet-flame decrees. And this is a reasonable precautionary measure. We simply limited access to this mighty instrument for those individuals who have not reached the necessary level of evolution of their consciousness, so as not to let them do much harm to themselves.

We simply took the matches away from the children.

The same is true for my dispensation on the 23rd of each month which allows the transmuting of the karma of the following month. It is also limited and functions selectively.

How can you define whether you are under the function of the dispensation or not? You can define it in accordance with your achievements on your Path. If a year ago, the same as two years ago, the same as ten years ago you were offended by people, condemned them and permitted other imperfections and if now you persistently continue doing it, then you can understand that this dispensation cannot be applied to you. However, nothing is lost irrevocably. If you truly decide to leave your unreal part and if you manifest your readiness to do it in your constant everyday aspirations, everything will return to you. You will feel the violet flame returning to your life and helping you get rid of your imperfection. In the end, everything is determined by your inner aspiration and your inner motive.

I would like to remind you that the reading of the decrees and prayers is not the most essential thing. The most essential is your wish to get rid of your ego and to serve life and God. This wish can be realised in any action and any situation you face in life.

Your usual actions, your attitudes to people and the surrounding world can work out karma just as well as reading the decrees. You make your choice at every moment of your life. And you either work out your previous karma through your actions or create a new one.

And any most perfect spiritual practice or the best prayers will be of no benefit to your spiritual evolution if you perform these practices with a mercenary aim to get some privileges for you or your relations.

There is only one true motive for a person starting any spiritual practice or any spiritual methodology. And that is to get rid of your ego and to approach God, to serve God and all the living creatures. If you start any spiritual practice with any other aim, you create karma.

The same principle of duality, inherent in your world, functions in the spiritual sphere and in the religious sphere. And sometimes a person, devout from the human point of view and regularly attending all church services and ceremonies, is on a lower step in his spiritual evolution than a person who never attends church services, but has a correct inner motive and realises in his life those Commandments which were taught by Jesus and other Teachers of mankind.

It will not be a big revelation if I say that there are many more spiritually advanced people outside the religious confessions than among the people acting in the frames of a certain religious system.

I have given you today enough information to think about. And I have taken advantage of the opportunity to give you the information about the changes which our previous dispensations have undergone so far.

I AM Surya from the Great Central Sun. Om

Just one of your vibrations of Love and Compassion is capable of extinguishing the fire of hell where many souls of this planet are burning now

Beloved Hilarion, April 10, 2005

I AM Hilarion, Lord of the Fifth Ray. I HAVE come to you through this Messenger.

I have come to inform you about some things which you face in life but to which you do not attach much importance. But if you scrutinise these things, it becomes clear that they will determine your life in the world for many years ahead.

I have come to tell you how you yourselves can create your own future. To some of you this information can seem unreal and unjust. Others may be familiar with it already. But I think it is always useful to remember and to repeat the lesson you have sometimes learnt.

So, I would like to dwell on the reasons for the spiritual and somatic ailments burdening your physical and higher bodies.

Man's memory is very short and, as a rule, it is very difficult for man to follow a direct link between the actions he performs in life and their consequences. But it is exactly this connection that is at the basis of the Law of Karma or so-called Law of Cause and Effect and Retribution.

Mother Mary and I have to listen to many humans asking for the healing of ailments. A person whose physical temple is stricken by a serious ailment is ready to make significant sacrifices so as to get rid of it. He seeks external healers, capable of helping him. Only after having seen a series of doctors and healers – who spread their hands helplessly and receive proper payment for it – does this person appeal to God and the Ascended Hosts for help.

The moment comes when mind prevails in man and he realises that the ailment was sent to him from heaven and that only God can liberate him from it. And man seeks paths to God; he is ready to make sacrifices and to read a lot of prayers so as to heal himself.

Hardly anybody understands that the ailments and suffering were caused not by an angry and vindictive God but by his own actions performed both in his previous lives and during his current embodiment.

When you are young and full of strength and energy you almost never think about the consequences of your actions. It seems natural to you to receive something that you wish for, even if you have to offend or insult somebody painfully.

How incommensurable sometimes is a wish you fight to satisfy with the harm which you are ready to do to others simply to satisfy your wish at any price.

Thus, your first and main enemy that is sometimes your only enemy is hidden inside of you. It is your carnal mind with its insatiable desires.

You think there is nothing awful in your fight to satisfy your wishes. It seems absolutely natural to you, especially in youth. You do not even attach any importance to obvious breaches of moral norms which you commit while satisfying your desires. You simply do not think about the harm you do to other people.

How can your insatiable passions be conquered? How can we put an end to your greed for the pleasures of life? Very few people are capable of learning by themselves, looking at examples of other people, reading books and finding people who can share their Wisdom with them.

For those who are not capable of understanding and learning, the Law of Karma or Retribution comes into force.

Each of your deeds committed in disagreement with the Will of God leads to the fact that the Divine Energy which you are using continuously and without which you are not able to exist is tainted with this imperfect deed. The more imperfect actions you perform, the lower the vibrations of the Divine Energy become. This energy does not disappear; it is kept in your aura, in your emotional, mental and etheric bodies. And this energy turns into a magnet attracting to itself similar energies from the external world surrounding you.

Therefore, if you have offended someone, this energy will attract to you a situation which will offend you sooner or later.

You carry in your aura records of all your imperfect deeds. These records are like holes in your aura. If you often allow yourself to perform actions which are to be punished due to the Law of Karma, sooner or later your aura becomes over-saturated with these negative vibrations. And you will no longer be able to work out your loads of karma by performing right deeds during those karmic situations which are sent to you in exchange for your previous deeds till the end of the current embodiment - too much negative energy has accumulated in your aura.

You have already been told that the time you live in is unique. It is the time when the change of cosmic cycles takes place and a new cycle begins.

People burdened with too much negative energy will be sick and will be deprived of an opportunity to be active in life. They will be denied the Divine Energy and an opportunity to go on multiplying their imperfections in this world. A person with an aura burdened with too great a quantity of negative energy is like a leper, an incurably sick and dangerous person. The negative vibrations of his aura are capable of inducing similar negative vibrations in the auras of all the people with whom he comes into contact.

Due to the law of likeness such people will be drawn to each other, and they already inhabit whole zones on planet Earth which can be compared with leprosaria for lepers.

If a person with a pure aura happens to be in such zones he feels like a fish thrown to the shore.

When we watch your planet we see these zones, these centres, as receptacles of negative energies, condensed to such an extent that not one of our healing rays sent by us tirelessly to the Earth is able to break through them.

People who have trapped themselves in these energetic leprosaria are not able to help themselves any more and need help that can still be rendered them from outside.

That is why we are ready for co-operation and we are ready to use everybody who is capable of keeping his vibrations at a level high enough for him to render help through himself to those people who seem already absolutely dead spiritually, but fasten their eyes on heaven in their last hope and sincerely plead and implore for help.

We are ready to help and we help everybody. This help may not concern the physical body which is already beyond the possibility of being restored due to the predominance of the irreversible processes in it. Our help concerns first of all the souls of these people. We are trying to heal and keep the souls of those who have fixed their eyes on heaven at least once in their life, sincerely asked for help and confessed to all the sins committed. There is no sinner without a future. But it is also fair that it is impossible to save those who themselves do not need this salvation.

Therefore, there is always a possibility to render help, though sometimes we lack sincere servants, ready to sacrifice themselves for the sake of mankind's salvation and for the sake of rendering help to all living creatures.

Now I am appealing to those who are capable of understanding me and who understand what I am talking about.

The time has come when war is being waged literally for every embodied soul. There are forces trying to keep as many souls as possible in the plane of illusion. And there are forces fighting literally for every soul in order to pull it out of hell which is now represented in the physical plane by many places on planet Earth.

And sometimes just one meeting, one loving and compassionate look is enough for a soul doomed for non-existence, to help it find Faith, Hope and Love.

Keep your balance, your mental peace. You are warriors in this world. And just one of your vibrations of Love and Compassion is capable of extinguishing the fire of hell in which many souls of this planet are burning now.

I AM Hilarion and I have appealed to the warriors of Spirit on this planet

You must find all the warriors of Light who are incarnated now and remind them about their mission

Lord Lanto, April 12, 2005

I AM LANTO, having come to you through this Messenger.

I HAVE come to have a very important and crucial conversation with you now. You know that every time we come to give a dictation, we try to offer you a piece of new information, but usually it is just a new point of view on the facts and information with which you are already familiar. Now I want to offer you absolutely new information, and this information will possibly seem unexpected and even fantastic to many of you.

So, I am beginning. You know me as the Lord of the Second Ray. This is the Ray of Wisdom and Illumination. So, my teaching will be delivered to you through this very Ray.

Imagine a person who has managed to neutralise all the negative karma accumulated in his bodies for many thousands of embodiments. The emotional, mental, etheric and physical bodies of such a person do not contain any energy which was misused by him during the entire cycle of his existence on planet Earth. What do you think will happen to this person? Will he be able to go on dwelling in the physical world or will he have to perform a transition so as to continue his existence in a higher world?

But are there people on planet Earth who have managed to neutralise all their karma?

You may justly say that apart from neutralising karma it is also necessary to carry out the Divine Plan. But the Divine Plan for every individual is completely coordinated with the Divine Plan for the whole planet Earth. And perhaps many of you have already guessed that most likely such a man will keep staying in embodiment. God's Plan is not aimed at enabling one particularly advanced individual to go on perfecting himself after separating himself completely from other living creatures and the entire universe. Therefore, if a person has managed to neutralise his personal karma, it does not mean at all that he can immediately perform a transition to the higher planes.

On the contrary, such a human becomes very important for God and the Ascended Hosts. He is no longer burdened by excessive karmic loads; his chakras are liberated from karmic rubbish and start conducting the Divine Energy in all its fullness.

Of course, if an individual wishes to perform the transition, his appeal will not be turned down. But in fact a person who has neutralised his personal karma up to 100% stops thinking in personal terms. He realises his unity with the entire universe, and he realises his entire unity with God. That is why such a person willingly grants his bodies for the carrying out of the Divine mission.

You know that in addition to personal karma, families, towns, countries and the world also have karma.

On the whole, the entire planet is surrounded now by very dense energies. These energies can be compared to a very dense crust shrouding the planet. It is necessary to dissolve this crust of negative energy. A person, having worked out his karma, takes upon himself obligations to transmute the planetary karma in the subtle planes. What is this process like?

When the aura of a person acquires the Divine Purity and his chakras conduct the Divine Energy into the world freely, such a person willingly starts to absorb negative energies from the surrounding world into his aura and to convert them. It can be compared to a vacuum cleaner. The person comes into contact with the auras of other people or with masses of negative energy drifting in the surrounding area, and with the help of his chakras starts neutralising this dense negative energetic substance.

Such people can be compared to Christ in their service to the world. As the vibrations of these people differ too much from the vibrations of the surrounding world, they perceive the very dwelling in the surrounding world as an endless daily crucifixion. They are really crucified on the cross between Spirit and Matter. Worlds join each other within the chakras of these people.

You know that human chakras bind the physical body with the higher bodies. So, when the chakras of a human are completely purified, such a man becomes similar to an open door between the worlds. The service of such a person is in this case similar to the service that Christ carried out while in incarnation. Such people sacrifice of their free will for the sake of the salvation of others.

Do you understand what I am speaking about, beloved? A person voluntarily chooses to stay amidst the densest energies of this world. But, as his vibrations differ too much from the vibrations of the surrounding world, the very act of staying among human beings is for him like a daily crucifixion on a cross. And this is a crucifixion indeed. Such a man takes upon himself the karma of the world, the sins of the world. He absorbs these sins and karma into his body and transmutes them by his service to the world and to all living creatures.

I give such a detailed description of this service because many of you render such a service to the world, but, possibly, do not even realise this with your external waking consciousness and physical mind. Each true lightbearer who is embodied now serves 24 hours a day, without sleep or rest.

That is because many of you go on serving during your sleep as well, in the astral plane in the higher bodies, to help purify this plane from negative energy. During this night labour your higher bodies receive real wounds. You get up in the morning and do not remember the night's heroic deeds and feel broken and weak, because the angel-healers did not have enough time to help your higher bodies during your night's sleep.

I want you to know about the service of your fellows and about your own service. Your work is invaluable in the eyes of God and the Ascended Hosts. And I feel uneasy asking you to take upon yourselves an additional burden. There are very few warriors of Light embodied on earth at present. Many of them have forgotten about their duty and yielded to the temptations of this world. They have forgotten what they have come into embodiment for.

That is why I ask you to find these warriors of Light and to remind them of their service and the duties they took upon themselves before coming into embodiment. Find them, give them these dictations to read, talk to them. Let it be a personal conversation or a public lecture. Each of you knows what you should do.

But you should find all the warriors of Light who are incarnated now and remind them about their mission.

I would like to thank you for your service. And I bow my head before God's Light beaming from within you.

I AM Lanto

The greatest among you is that one who serves others most of all

Beloved Vairochana, April 16, 2005

I AM Vairochana, having come through this messenger.

I AM a Buddha of one of the Secret Rays, and I belong to the Mandala of the Five Dhyani Buddhas[1].

I AM also a member of the Karmic Board.

I am to give you some knowledge concerning the Secret Rays today.

You know, perhaps, that in addition to the seven basic rays corresponding to the seven basic chakras located along the spinal column, there are also secret rays.

You know from the teachings of the past that the secret rays' chakras are focused on the palms, feet and in the place which was pierced with a spear when Jesus was on the cross.

Perhaps, not everybody knows that apart from the seven basic chakras along the spine, there are other chakras alternating with the basic ones. These are also the secret rays' chakras.

My chakra is the one located between the solar plexus chakra and the heart chakra. I point at this chakra with a gesture of my hands when I am portrayed as a statue.

Today I would like to give a certain teaching concerning the chakra located in the centre of the chest.

---

[1] To the initiate, the mandala of the Five Dhyani Buddhas represents both a cosmic diagram of the world and of himself. It is a tool for spiritual growth and mystical experience – a map to enlightenment saturated with divine possibilities. (translator's footnote)

This is the central chakra, and this chakra is activated only in people who have a great level of merit in their past which is confirmed in the current embodiment. This chakra connects you straight with your I AM Presence. This is the chakra of Buddhas and Bodhisattvas.

A person having received access to this chakra's energies can use its help of his own will and transmute not only his karma, but the karma of the world.

That is why Buddhas and Bodhisattvas are said to serve the world and to transmute the karma of the world.

Buddhas' prayers are chakras' pulsation. Buddha's prayers become achievable only for those individuals who have balanced their karma up to 100 % and made a vow to serve mankind.

Every Buddha who is embodied now bears on his shoulders an enormous piece of the planetary karma. That is why many individuals who have achieved the level of a Buddha's consciousness aspire to be embodied in the physical body, to pass through the necessary initiations so as to activate their chakras and to serve the world with the help of Buddha's prayers.

Many Buddhas are embodied on earth now. And each of such Buddhas purifies from karma a space for many hundreds and even thousands of kilometres around him through his self-sacrificing service. The service of such a Buddha substitutes the service of tens of thousands of pure monks and virtuous people.

You are not able to define the level of merit of a Buddha with your human consciousness. But every such Buddha, when meeting an embodied brother-in-service and communicating with him for just a few minutes, is able to recognise familiar and close vibrations manifested in everything – in the tone of the voice, gestures, even in the way of dressing and behaving.

The main problem which the Buddhas in embodiment face in their life is the dense and low vibrations of the surrounding world. They cannot practically be in large cities among masses of people. That is why they choose solitary dwelling places in overgrown parts and in the mountains. However, the basic principle of such Buddhas' service is the enlightenment of mankind. Therefore, they meet with people and give them their teaching as far as their external circumstances allow.

But many of them still never meet with ordinary people till the end of their life, so as to stay in the places where their chakras can work with all their might and pass Light into the dense physical world.

Today I have partly unveiled information connected with the service of the Ascended Hosts to ordinary people whom they even do not see. It would be strange, if at this difficult time for the Earth the Ascended Hosts relied only on the prayers of neophytes making their first scarcely visible steps on their Path leading them back to God. Their steps are so hesitant and unsteady; at times the surrounding illusion carries them away so completely that they forget about both God and their Path.

But let us not judge these people sternly. Each of them is on his own part of the Path, and each of them does his best according to his level of merit.

In fact, these neophytes do not bear any significant karmic responsibility for their actions, sometimes even seriously wrong ones. Such actions lead to the multiplication of the illusion and are expressed in performing too many external rituals that divert people's attention from the essence of the Teaching about God.

However, there are people who have achieved a significant level of merit on their Path and who consciously use their achievements for receiving external signs of power and authority. They manipulate neophytes who suspect nothing and even use the energy of prayers for their mercenary purposes. These people create a heavy karma, which will be followed by a just karmic retribution.

The higher your level of merit is, the greater karmic responsibility you undertake when receding from the Path and leading others from this Path.

Therefore, the only way for people sincerely aspiring to God to see the danger from these false shepherds is to purify their bodies, thoughts and feelings so as to obtain a clear vision and the gift of recognition which will allow them to understand who is who.

I am fully aware of the fact that it is too hard to make such identification with your external consciousness. But I assure you that in your soul you always know who is a true bearer of the Divine Energy, and who only picks the light of others and lives at the expense of this light.

Having received this knowledge from your soul, you simultaneously face up to the karmic responsibility for using your light in support of such false shepherds.

You have understood my thought. Only such a person bears a karmic responsibility for his false usage of light that has recognised false shepherds, but still goes on giving his light in their support due to reasons connected with his ego.

But if a false teacher leads innocent people from the true Path, even I would not like to use my abilities to foresee the consequences of the karma created by him.

Today I have given you the knowledge about true servants, and I have given you the understanding of false service.

And having received this knowledge, you will not be able to choose your teachers irresponsibly any longer. Watch and observe. In doubtful situations you can always make a sincere appeal to the Ascended Hosts or to the Lord who is closest to you and to whom you feel a deep inner affinity and link, and you will receive help. One nice day you will be given a vision, and you will see the inner essence of the teacher whom you follow.

You just need to trust your Higher Part more. Oh, you are much more than the reflection you see in front of you in the mirror every day. In reality you are mighty spiritual beings who have come into this world to obtain a human experience. It was your soul who chose the circumstances of your current embodiment even before it began.

And you knew that no matter how hard your Path would be, you would accomplish the mission undertaken to expand the consciousness of people around you.

I have come today to awaken the memory of your soul about the responsibilities which it undertook before the current embodiment.

So leave aside the toys you play with even after having matured to adulthood. It is time to become adults, to raise your consciousness up to the level of a mature person and to undertake responsibility not only for yourselves but for those whose level of consciousness is lower than yours.

Remember that the greatest among you is that one who serves others most of all. The greatest servant of mankind is a Buddha sitting meekly in the pose of meditation in the mountains and transmuting the world's karma with the help of his chakras.

I do not ask you to sit in the pose of meditation and to try to transmute the world's karma. Each of you was born exactly in that very place, in that country and in the midst of those external circumstances which you must use for your achievements, and the people and circumstances around you are exactly those that need your help.

I am leaving you alone with your thoughts about the directions you have received today.

I AM Vairochana and I have been with you today

You should become electrodes through which the physical plane of planet Earth will be saturated with Light

Beloved Pallas Athena, April 17, 2005

I AM Pallas Athena, having come to you through this messenger. Do you know me? I AM the Goddess of Truth and I AM a member of the Karmic Board as well.

I HAVE come to you today to give you certain knowledge about the manifestation of the Law of Karma in your physical world. When you come into embodiment, a veil is drawn behind you and you forget about the events you lived through before the embodiment; you forget your previous embodiments. Such a state of affairs has not been forever. But this measure is rather more humane than restricting with respect to your lifestreams.

The point is that in the course of your numerous lives you performed actions that were not the best ones. And if you remembered all your past grave actions and abuses, you would not be able to function in your current life. Therefore, the veil of your memory is drawn just after you are born. However, this veil is not thick for those who, due to their merits, have woven the way for obtaining the gift of seeing the past and the future. You know that many prophets and saints, embodied on Earth in the past and in the present, had the gift of second-sight.

The veil rises slightly when your four lower bodies obtain a certain level of purity and your consciousness rises up to the level at which it is not frightened by some phenomena taking place at the moment of the interaction of the worlds. In reality the human consciousness is very limited. It is limited by the role you perform in your current life and by the karma you created during your previous lives. It is your karma in fact that causes an obstruction between you and the higher planes. Your karma is energy, a thick energetic substance with a very low frequency of vibrations.

And these low frequency vibrations are that very veil that separates you from our world.

Therefore, beloved, there is no difference between you and me except the difference in our vibrations. And when an opportunity comes for you to get rid of your karma and imperfections due to your efforts and merits, you are able to communicate with our world and to dwell in it. Your range of world-perception is broadened and you acquire many abilities called the gifts of the Holy Spirit.

That is why the target of my talk today is to give you a more correct understanding of the fact that only you yourselves with your actions in the past and present have created this veil separating you from the Real World of God. But, as due to God's plan everything in this world develops in an evolutionary way, the next stage you reach will inevitably be the stage of liberating your earthly embodiments from karma.

You get rid of your karma and rise to a higher energetic level.

In reality you can get rid of your karma in a few ways. You can make the right choices. Your life is nothing else but a chain of situations in which you are always given a chance to select one of two choices. One of them advances you to God, while the other one estranges you from Him. Everything is very simple. And all the multiplicity of life situations can be condensed down to just these two choices.

And this path is the only one followed by all people embodied on earth. All the other paths are just supporting ones.

This path is familiar to you as a prayer-practice when, with the momentum of your heart, you start attracting additional Divine Energy into your life and, with the help of this Energy, further dissolve your karmic burdens.

You have been told recently about a higher practice of dissolving karma with the help of chakras' pulsation.[2] I'm sorry to say that this practice becomes accessible only when your level of spiritual merit is high enough.

But the main task for you is just to fulfil your aspiration to overcome that limited state in which you are dwelling because of karma. If you know the diagnosis, it is easier for you to find the correct treatment and to apply it in your life.

That is why everything you do in life is a way of overcoming your limited karmic state. That is the purpose in coming to embodiment.

Such is the Law of this world. There was a time when you made a choice to test yourselves in embodiment as individuals. You were granted freedom to perform your experiments. And you started to use the Divine Energy of your choice. For this purpose each of you was endowed with a personality. Your personality was given a mind at a certain stage of evolutionary development. But the mind has a quality of duality. It has an opportunity to choose how to use its abilities.

---

[2] See: the dictations "You must find all the warriors of light who are incarnated now and remind them about their mission" *Lord Lanto, April 12, 2005* and "The greatest among you is that one who serves others most of all" *Beloved Vairochana, April 16, 2005*

As a result of your experiments with your mind you began shrouding yourselves with thicker and thicker energies, creating karma, i.e. using the Divine Energy not in harmony with the plan of God, but in accordance with the plan of your own mind.

Your activity in the lower physical world during millions of years has created the surrounding reality you are living in now. You know that the world surrounding you is just a mirror reflecting your imperfect consciousness. That was the stage when, in accordance with the plan of God for this universe, you were allowed to experiment with the Divine Energy of your own free will.

Now a new stage is approaching. During the first stage you plunged into the illusion, but now the stage of your return to the Real Wold of God has come.

In accordance with God's plan those souls who took part in the creation of the illusion have to overcome this illusory manifestation through their actions. And first of all you must give up your imperfect creation in your consciousness.

At the first stage you must plunge into the matter deeper and deeper and thus separate yourself from God more and more. At the second stage you must return to the real part of yourself. This can happen after you have given up the illusion and turned to the reality and after you have understood your Unity with God.

While overcoming your imperfect state and working out your karma you raise your vibrations. The rise of your vibrations simultaneously causes the rise of the surrounding world vibrations.

You overcome yourselves, overcome your human nature and obtain more and more Divine qualities, returning step by step to the Divine Reality from whence your souls have come into the physical world to experiment.

The dictations given through this messenger are destined for the awakening of the memory of your souls and for giving your aspirations the right direction.

In the course of your evolution you obtain a more correct vision step by step, and you recognise the Divine Truth and become United with this Truth at a certain stage.

Today I have tried to give you a slightly different point of view on the changes taking place on earth now.

In fact, all the changes are possible and will become possible only due to your help, due to the aspirations of your hearts and due to the Divine Energy which you pass into your lower world.

And in the nearest future you, who are reading these lines, should become electrodes through which the physical plane of planet Earth will be saturated with Light.

I wish you to succeed on this path and to overcome the obstacles within you, which prevent you from implementing God's plan for this planet.

I AM Pallas Athena

The best sermon will be your personal example

The Goddess of Liberty, April 22, 2005

I AM the Goddess of Liberty, having come to you through this messenger. I AM a member of the Karmic Board and I have come to you with a definite purpose on the eve of April 23rd.

Beloved Surya came to you on March 19th to tell you that the monthly dispensation on the 23rd of each month is active now only for the souls with pure hearts and pure motives of actions. Therefore, don't forget that on the 23rd of each month you have an opportunity to transmute your karma of the following month.

I AM the Goddess of Liberty. First of all, the quality of Divine Freedom is determined for you by freedom from your karma and from the energies you distorted in the past by your actions not corresponding to God's Will. These energies tie you down to the physical plane and to other dense layers of planet Earth. So, your main task is to liberate yourselves from these ties.

The process of liberation cannot be instantaneous. If all the energies distorted by you during many thousands of incarnations were activated in your aura all of a sudden, you would not be able to endure such a load. Therefore, in accordance with the humane Law of Cosmic Cycles your life is divided into time intervals, during which one or another distorted energy is activated. These time intervals are a multiple of the 12 basic rays of the Cosmic clock. These time cycles are divided into annual cycles, so called 12-year cycles, in accordance with the Zodiac signs, and further into monthly cycles within every year.

These are the cycles, in agreement with which you get into such karmic situations that you need to pass in order to neutralise energies distorted by you earlier and still contained in your aura.

Everything in the universe takes place in accordance with the cosmic cycles, and these cycles were written by God in the language of stars. A person who manages to master this language will get access to the details of God's plan for the entire universe and for a concrete planet or a star. At the moment of your birth the Cosmic clock of your lifestream is initiated. The spring of your individual clock is wound up. Knowing the plan of your life, which is also determined by stars at the moment of your birth, you may know which energies from your previous karmic records become accessible for working out and what time periods will be assigned for that.

If you scrutinise your life attentively, you may notice that exactly the same problems, connected with your state of mind and your perception of yourself and the surrounding world, crop up in front of you with enviable periodicity. The spring keeps unwinding, and with each of its circles the same problems return to you with enviable constancy. And again you have to return to the qualities you have not worked out to solve life problems cropping up in front of you each time at a new level.

All this resembles ocean waves lapping against the shore. A wave runs over the shore and then recedes. While moving, a wave embroils stones lying on the shore of the ocean and carries them away. After thousands of years stones become smooth. Any roughness is polished by the ocean. In the very same way God polishes your imperfect qualities day after day, year after year, in accordance with the Law of

Cosmic Cycles, until you become smooth and your aura acquires the right oval form, the transparency and the tints that were inherent in your soul primordially before you undertook your embodiment in the physical world. This process of polishing your qualities and transforming them into the Divine ones lasts for many lives.

A wise man understands that it is impossible to pass by the force of the Cosmic Law, but the result to which this Law directs you may be achieved during a shorter period of time, if you do not resist the Law, but help to observe it. In this case you may achieve results during fewer cosmic cycles. All this explains the meaning of the saying that the days of the chosen people will be shortened.

You have an opportunity to shorten the days of your life on Earth only if you speed up the returning of your karma. While an ordinary person will need tens of years to work out his karma, you will be able to do it in a year. You will just transform the distorted energy faster owing to your own wish and the Divine mercy which enables you to do it.

Therefore, don't close your eyes to the 23rd date of each month. If your intentions are good, you can transmute your karma of the following month during this day not only by making correct choices, but also with the help of the practice of praying. I would like you to know the right motive with which you should start reading prayers on such a day:

- You sincerely realise all your sins committed in the past and try to do all that is within your power not to commit them in the future.

- With the help of the impetus of your hearts, filled with love towards the entire Creation and every living creature, you are ready to attract to your world such an amount of the Divine Energy which will let you completely transform the energy distorted by you.

In this way, if you are able to transform into Light all the distorted energy, which is open for transformation at this cosmic term, and if you do it with the help of thc achicvcd impetus and in accordance with the law, then when the next period comes you will have nothing to transform.

Yet, you will continue your serving, because as long as you are in embodiment, you must use every minute of your stay on Earth for helping all the living creatures that are not as successful in their movement on the Path as you.

In order for a human to realise his position in this world, to see his imperfection and to aspire to God, he needs initial energy, enabling him to do this.

Imagine that you came up to a person, so heavily overburdened with karma that he does not realise his connection with God and all the other creatures on Earth. He is like a sooty pot, too sooty. Why not use a part of your energy to rub this pot? Why not clean it with a duster, to help it get at least a little particle of the Divine energy, a tiny ray of Light capable of awakening the sleeping consciousness of this person?

If you can remember, each of you was in such a sooty state in the past. And there always happened to be a person who glanced at you tenderly or expressed compassion towards your soul. And you received the portion of energy you were lacking at that moment, so you could raise your consciousness up to the level of comprehension of a higher Reality. Each of you needs help and each of you can offer such help.

You can give help unconsciously, with your glance, with your reaction to some stirred up critical situation. The best sermon will be your personal example, your behaviour in life, your attitude to life situations and tests.

Your final exam at the primary school of initiations will be the day when you see how many people around you need your help. And your biggest achievement will be the moment when you are sincerely happy with the achievements of your fellow-brothers. When you are genuinely happy with the success of the people around you, you will receive all their achievements as an impetus of your own gains.

In this way you can multiply your treasures in heaven, the treasures of your causal body. You may do nothing at all but only help others and be sincerely happy with the achievements of others. And you will make much more merit and good karma, than even when you fight with your own personal weaknesses with all your might.

Today I have revealed to you a very simple secret, owing to which many people deserved their ascension and put an end to the chain of their earthly embodiments. Be able to be happy with the achievements of other people and to admire their merits.

I AM the Goddess of Liberty, and I have given you my exhortations today

I will enter your temples and act through you

Beloved El Morya, April 28, 2005

I AM El Morya, having come to you again through my messenger.

I HAVE come to you to affirm new knowledge and understanding of the events taking place in the subtle plane of planet Earth now. You know that the cycles are changing now. Many words were told about that both in the dictations given through this messenger and in the dictations given by us through other messengers.

What characterises the present stage of the transformations happening on Earth now and connected with the changing of the cycles?

You will be surprised if I tell you that the transformations in the subtle plane have been practically completed. All the layers of the subtle plane, with the exception of the lowest astral layers, have been purified by us from those negative energies which managed to penetrate to the layers that were not inherent in their essence. It was grandiose work, beloved, and it has been completed by us effectively.

Now the phase has come when we start, properly speaking, purifying the layers close to the physical plane and purifying the very physical plane as well.

What is the difficulty? The forces that managed to penetrate illicitly to the layers with high vibrations are now pressed down to Earth by us. And they look for any pretext to strengthen their positions in the physical plane and in the densest layers of the astral plane. These forces do not have their own source of the Divine Energy, and they feed on your energy which you grant at their full disposal so thoughtlessly at times.

Therefore, the question of the checking of the spending of the Divine Energy appears in the foreground now. The leitmotiv of almost all these dictations, if you reread them attentively, is just the control over the expenditure of the Divine Energy which you, beloved, must perform by yourselves.

Each of you is a source of the Divine Energy for your physical world. You choose yourselves – as the creatures endowed with the free will - where to spend the Energy granted you by God.

It is impossible for you not to spend this energy. Every minute and every second of your living on Earth the Divine Energy comes into your aura as a continuous flow from the Divine world. And it depends only on you how you will use your Divine Energy.

The forces of darkness do not have access to the Divine Energy, but they are very experienced in the tricks of misappropriation of your Divine Energy. They take the energy you grant them so thoughtlessly through any non-divine actions that you let yourselves perform in your world.

The entire modern industry devotes 90 % of its activity to the satisfying of the energetic needs of the forces of darkness. Have you ever thought about it, beloved? It seems harmless to you to go to a concert of rock-music, to see horror-films, soap operas, films contributing to the violence propaganda.

It seems inoffensive if you, following fashion, buy things which are absolutely unnecessary for you. Each thing which you buy contains certain vibrations inside it. There are things bringing the Light, and there are things taking your Light from you. Do you think about this when you spend your money - an equivalent of your Divine Energy - on the purchasing of non-divine things? Do you ask for advice of your Christ Self when making your purchases?

Every moment of your life you make a choice, and this choice directs your Divine Energy either onto the multiplication of the illusion of this world or onto its contraction.

You tint your Divine Energy with beautiful feelings full of joy and love, and you raise the vibrations of this world. But when you are full of negative thoughts and feelings, you fill this world with heavy energy, viscous trcaclc of your negativity.

Only you can establish control over every erg of the Divine Energy spent by you. We cannot do it for you. We desire each of you to turn into an electrode of Light, filling the world around you with the vibrations of harmony, beauty, love and joy. And we undertake a responsibility to help each of you who will truly want to help us in our work on the purification of your octave from the forces of darkness. But we cannot force you to make your choice, beloved.

We offer you a very simple decision, not requiring of you any additional time that is usually necessary for prayer-reading, though the prayers are now necessary as never before, being an extra source of Light for the physical octave.

But if you constantly keep control over yourself and over the spending of your Divine Energy, it will not require any extra expenditure from you. On the contrary, it will help you save your financial resources. If you think over the question of where you spend your money, it will be clear that 90 % of the things and food which you purchase are absolutely unnecessary for the maintenance of your physical body. On the contrary, they help to ruin your body, and you become dependent on the whole industry which involves you first into the process of the destruction of your physical body and your psyche, and then courteously offers you an immense set of expensive methods by which you can restore your health.

Keep control over yourself during the day. Watch your thoughts, your feelings. Your thoughts give the direction for the flow of your energy. Analyse what you think about. If you think about the unjust government, you send your energy to the members of your government. If you think about your boss mistreating you at work, you send him your energy. If you think about the plot of the soap-opera you watched before, you send your energy on the multiplication of the whole egregore of artificial thoughts and feelings in the astral plane.

You are responsible for every erg of energy wasted by you thoughtlessly. Every time you waste your energy not in accordance with the Divine principles you create karma. And if you are aware of the karmic law but still go on violating the Divine principles to please your ego, your karma‘s character becomes much heavier.

Believe me, we never say our words without a purpose. And we do not spend our energy in vain. Every word told in these dictations through this messenger is directed exactly to giving you the knowledge which you need most at this moment.

That is why we do not become tired of repeating to you one and the same thing: you are responsible for the spending of your energy, and you are twice as responsible for the spending of your energy if you continue your way of life after the reading of these dictations and persuade yourself that nothing told in them concerns you in any way.

You are in embodiment in the physical octave, and before being embodied many of you undertook upon yourselves the duties of helping mankind in this hardest time of the changeover. And now we remind you about the responsibilities undertaken. Do not say then, when you appear in front of the Karmic Board, that you knew nothing and guessed about nothing, that you were not warned and you heard nothing.

I repeat it to you again and again. You have run out of time for learning. You are required to perform concrete actions and concrete steps in the physical plane.

It is hardly possible to formulate our demands to you more clearly than was done through this messenger. You should alter the priorities of your consciousness.

Remember, that we are powerless to do anything in your physical plane without your help and support. We have no access to your physical world, unless some of you prepare your temples for our presence and ask us to use your four lower bodies so that we can use your hands and feet for the implementing of our plans.

Thus, I give you this appeal. Please, make it every day.

"In the name of I AM THAT I AM, in the name of my mighty I AM Presence, in the name of my Holy Christ Self I appeal to beloved El Morya to enter my temple and act through me so that the Will of God can be manifested in the physical octave and in the densest layers of the astral plane. Beloved El Morya, I grant all my four lower bodies at your full disposal: the physical body, the astral body, the mental body and the etheric body. Act through me if there is God's Holy Will for that. Let God's Will be done. Amen."

I promise to you that as soon as an opportunity occurs I will enter your temples and act through you.

And thus we will change this world! And the Earth will live and become a beautiful star of liberty, joy and love!

I AM El Morya and I have given this message from the point of the highest Love towards you

You can receive at your disposal the mightiest tool of God

Beloved El Morya, April 29, 2005

I AM El Morya, having come to you!

I HAVE come to give you a small Teaching connected with the opportunity you acquire when all your four lower bodies and your chakras become pure.

You know that the four lower bodies of most people living on Earth now are in an extremely impure state.

And as far as you know that your chakras link your lower bodies among themselves and with the Divine world, it means that your chakras are also a very sorry sight.

Therefore, I have intended today to give you a certain Teaching connected with the opportunities which you acquire when your chakras are pure. And the abstract talks about the purification of your four lower bodies and about the purity of your chakras will sound more practical for you.

Thus, your chakras. You know that you have seven major chakras located along the spinal column, and you also have the secret rays' chakras, located along the spine as well, and you have many more chakras focused on many parts of your body. You know that there is a total of 144 chakras. 12 chakras transmit the perfect God-qualities to your world through the 12 Cosmic Rays, and each of these qualities bears in itself 12 more shades or half-tones. And when your chakras open like fascinating flowers, you become conductors of the perfect God-qualities into your physical reality.

God foresaw in advance all the possible abuses which mankind could carry out by wasting the Divine Energy. Therefore, when you misuse the Divine Energy from the point of view of the Divine Law governing in this universe, this affects first of all the capacity of your chakras. The Divine Energy flowing into your bodies along the crystal cord is limited naturally. This resembles a tap through which the Divine Energy streams into the physical world and which is first slightly turned off and finally turned off completely. And your possibilities of abusing the Divine Energy are cut down.

That is why the state of consciousness inherent in mankind at the present stage of its evolution cannot have at its disposal the unlimited Divine might. It is because the first thing your consciousness would do having received access to the unlimited source of the Divine Energy, would be to misuse this energy for satisfying the needs of its ego. But you know that the needs of your ego are impossible to satisfy. They are limitless.

Therefore, the access to the Divine Energy is reliably closed for most of mankind. In order to receive access to the Divine Energy you have to choose the Path of initiations. And this Path lasts for not only one life. In exceptional cases and only for our selected chelas we allow this Path to be passed during one life.

You are given tests or trials for each of the God-qualities. And you must pass each of these tests 12 times. You have to pass 144 tests in total for the successful finishing of the initiations on the 12 chakras, which is necessary for them to be open. If it were not for the returning tests which you have to pass due to your negligence, you could have achieved success during just a few years.

What does the opening of your chakras give you? Why do you need to aspire to it? A person having at his disposal such a mighty tool as open chakras can provide the world with invaluable service. And the major part of this service is in the purification of the surrounding world from any negative vibration and negative energies.

The might of your chakras is able to neutralise an utterly unimaginable quantity of the falsely qualified energy with which your world is literally saturated.

When you, beloved, utter your decrees or prayers, you attract additional Light into your world. This Light goes into your world through your chakras. Now imagine how much more Light you would be able to conduct into your world if your chakras were fully open. But at the moment when all your chakras are open you will have become a perfect Buddha - that is you reach the level of consciousness of Buddha in your own consciousness. Then, you cannot admit even into your thoughts anything that can do the slightest harm to the world and the living creatures around you.

You are constantly in the praying state of consciousness. But you do not even have to utter the words of your prayer in order to stay in the praying state of consciousness all the time. And at times your chakras even work independently of your consciousness like a vacuum cleaner, drawing into themselves all the rubbish from the world around you and filling this world with an irreproachably pure Divine Energy.

Therefore, when your chakras are open, you can appeal to your I AM Presence by asking it to direct the energy of your chakras for the resolving of this or that situation in your world. And if your asking is in correspondence with the Law of God, your I AM Presence will run the work of your chakras itself and the energy will be directed to the concrete situation about which you ask in your appeal.

You can use the energy of your throat chakra to protect yourself and also to protect all those whom you have the right to protect in accordance with God's Law.

You can transmute the karma with help of your chakras, not only your own karma, as by that moment you will not have your personal karma, but the karma of the planet and of the country. You may give your direct help to the people who need it and who ask you for help. This means actually fantastic opportunities and invaluable help to mankind, which you can give if you pass the necessary initiations for the opening of your chakras.

In order to understand better the might which comes to your disposal in this case, I will give you the following example.

Ten minutes of pulsation of your central chakra transmuting the karma will substitute the uttering of the violet flame decrees during 400 hours. This is really the mightiest tool, beloved, and this tool is hidden inside of you.

Today's talk was aimed at revealing to you the perspectives and opportunities of the next step. Beloved, many of you are ready for this step and still many are half--way to the full opening of your chakras.

You should know to what to aspire and what is your next step. You will receive at your disposal the might which is under the absolute control of your I AM Presence. And if you attempt to use this might not in accordance with the Will of God, your chakras simply will not pulsate. But if you still find a way to get round the Cosmic Law and to use the Divine Energy for your own purposes, your chakras will close and you will be refused access to the Divine Energy in the visible future.

God is ready to give you the most perfect tool, so necessary for you at this difficult time for planet Earth. Take it. Use it. But it depends only on you, beloved, whether you will or will not receive this perfect tool at your disposal. I tell you: the time has come; you can receive this mightiest tool of God at your disposal.

You only need to make a choice, to aspire to the Path of initiations, and to pass with honour each of the initiations which God will let you pass.

I AM El Morya and I will meet you on the Path of initiations

A teaching of the energy of the Divine Mother

Beloved Paul the Venetian, May 12, 2005

I AM Paul the Venetian, having come to you.

I AM the Master of the Third Ray, the Ray of Love. You can hardly find so many distortions on the other rays as we meet on the Ray of Love on earth. And it is quite explainable. If all the rest of the God-qualities were distorted by the dual state of the world, but only the quality of Divine Love were preserved in its primordial shape, the whole world would have another appearance. Love, the quality of Love, true Love, Divine Love – is catastrophically lacking in your world now.

I have come to affirm Love. I have come to impart Love to you.

The worlds are created by Love, and the worlds collapse due to the lack of the quality of Love. It is time you should think about Love and its manifestations in your life in real earnest. In reality the heart chakra which passes the energies of Love into your physical world is completely blocked in the majority of people. Therefore, you are short of Love and you try to compensate for its shortage by strange practices stimulating a pure physiological instinct. Trust me that the majority of distortions of the Divine Energy in your world are connected exactly with the misuse of the energy of the Divine Mother or, in other words, your sexual energy.

God endowed you with the Sacred Fire, the Flame of the Sacred Fire, which makes you similar to Gods. And believe me, this flame and this energy were given to you not for your pleasure. The more thoughtlessly you use your Sacred Fire, the more karma you create.

Your mass media and your stereotypes of behaviour in your society, even your way of behaving and dressing stimulate the misuse of your sexual energy. In the course of time you will be able to understand the authentic intention of the Sacred Fire granted to you by God.

But now you ought to understand that every time you use this gift not in accordance with the Divine intention you create karma. You create karma as you waste the Divine Energy for receiving shallow and purely animal pleasures. However, animals act much more reasonably than you in this respect. Their use of sexual energy happens at least in the framework of yearly cycles at an appropriate season of the year.

During an act of sexual intercourse a gigantic amount of the Divine Energy is released. This release of the Divine Energy can be compared with a flash of a hypernova star. And you know that your energy flows exactly in the same direction as your attention. And if at the moment of release of the Divine Energy you think of receiving pleasure for yourself and your partner, you use your sexual energy wrongly. Many of you will find my words impossible to absorb into your consciousness. I am absolutely aware that my words will sound strange to many of you. But I must inform you about the very elementary bases of the Divine Ethics which are known even to animals but have been forgotten by mankind for some reasons.

Everything in this world belongs to God. And you are particles of God. Therefore, everything you do, all your actions must conform to the Divine Law and take place within the framework of this Law. If you do something against the Will of God, you violate the Law of this universe and create karma. Thus, no matter how strange my instructions and recommendations seem to you, please simply listen to them from the beginning.

Before an act of sexual intercourse, please, bring your actions into line with the Will of God. You must be in lawful wedlock with your sexual partner. You must never have homosexual intercourse or sexual intercourse with accidental partners. Why is it so necessary to be in lawful wedlock with a constant partner? The point is that during the performing of your matrimonial duty a direct exchange of energy between your partner and you takes place. Communicating with people, you constantly exchange energies, but your energy exchange during sexual intercourse is multiplied greatly. In fact, you exchange all your energies – both good and bad ones. You take upon yourselves the karma of each other and you share your merits with your sexual partners. And if you are in lawful wedlock, then during your mutual life you have an opportunity to work out not only your own karma, but also the karma of your spouse, if the latter outbalances yours.

Now imagine that you are engaged in sexual intercourse with many partners. And imagine that the percent of the karma they have worked out is much less than yours. And their karmic loads can be much heavier than yours. They might have come to this world to work out their karma of a murder, of a betrayal or of some other dire kinds of karma. And when you absolutely thoughtlessly have sexual intercourse with them, you take upon yourself a part of their karma. And if at the same time you are in lawful wedlock, you take this karma upon your family. And how can you be shocked when all your life problems crop up after that?

Sexual energy has the same nature as the energy used for creation in your world. And when you waste your sexual potential for pleasure, you deprive yourself of creative energy and limit your evolution. In reality, such an abuse of the sexual energy results in the absolute incapability of the majority of people for the higher creative activity because they are too devastated when they approach maturity. They are simply incapable of becoming co-creators with God and of performing any creative work in your world.

The purpose of my dictation today is to raise a very important question before you. I am doing it as openly and as frankly as possible, because I repeat again that it is exactly through the abuse of the energy of the Divine Mother that the greatest part of the energy is distorted by mankind.

Every act of intercourse within wedlock should be performed in the name of God. Pray to God and dedicate the Sacred Fire released during your sexual intercourse, to God. Remember that your energy flows exactly in the same direction as your attention. And if you dedicate the release of your Sacred Fire to God, you will direct all the freed energy into the higher spheres of Light. And this energy will return to you afterwards as blessings for you and your children.

Try to use the Energy of the Divine Mother only for the aim of conceiving children. If at first it is difficult for you to be confined to such limitations, try to cut down the number of your acts of intercourse to once or twice a week.

Do not forget to direct all the released energy to God at least in an unspoken wish. Ask God to use this energy for blessing you, your children and your whole family.

Always remember that all your actions in the physical plane can be used both for the good and for the evil. Every minute and every second of your life in the physical world you receive the Divine Energy and you either direct it for the creation of the illusion - when it forms a sediment in this world and multiplies the illusion - or you send it towards the Divine world, creating a good karma and multiplying your treasures and merits in Heaven. The use of your sexual energy should be the corner-stone of your life.

I would like you to thoroughly familiarise yourselves with my lecture today and to try to apply all my recommendations in your life.

I AM Paul the Venetian

Try to keep the state of inner peace and harmony during most of the day

Beloved Kuthumi, May 19, 2005

I AM Kuthumi, having come to you again. I have come today to give you a small Teaching which may probably seem unexpected to you, but I would still like you to familiarise yourselves carefully with everything which I consider necessary to bring to your consciousness at this stage.

As you know, the event which took place at the end of last year – an earthquake and a tsunami – was utterly and completely caused by the imperfect consciousness of mankind. With surprising doggedness humanity continues to give birth to monstrous masses of negative energies which have wrapped the entire globe with a thick envelope. This envelope prevents the penetration of the renewal energies. In other words, a tension has been created between the forces which strive to keep the existing state on the planet and the forces striving to contribute to the implementation of the evolutionary plan for planet Earth.

On the one hand, you witness the constant and undeviating rise of the vibrations of the planet. On the other hand, an enormous amount of negative energy is still produced with the help of mass consciousness and the old stereotypes deeply ingrained in the consciousness of people. Where does the negative energy come from?

The whole energy of this universe is concentrated in the only source, and that is the Divine Energy. This energy comes to you along the crystal string, and you use it of your own free will. If you waste this energy to satisfy any of your egoistic strivings or to maintain negative thoughts, features or bad habits of a lifetime, it means that you vote for the obsolete way of living. You direct your energy to the strengthening of the masses of negative energy on this planet.

Therefore, when the positive renewal energy meets with the negative energy produced by humanity, this can be compared with a clash of two clouds with different charges. You know what happens when such clouds collide. You can observe thunder and lightning. Something similar to that is taking place on planet Earth at present. When two masses of energies with opposite potential clash, various disasters, natural calamities and hurricanes happen.

It may seem to you that the natural elements are blind and indomitable. But it is not quite true. As a rule, we manage to localise the masses of negative energy at the places where they appear. That is why only the areas which contribute to the production of the negative energetic masses with their consciousness suffer from the natural calamities.

Beloved, it is high time to part with the point of view that you may commit sins, act in improper ways, think and feel in ways unpleasing to God during most of the day, and be sure that after that you can sit down, pray and transmute the karma which you and your nearest and dearest have created.

There is no doubt that the worth of prayers is unquestionable, indisputable and unarguable. The effectiveness of prayers is beyond discussion. But it is not enough just to pray in this situation, beloved. What is the point of producing negative energetic masses at first and then fighting against them?

It is time for you to approach everything you do during the day consciously. You should constantly control your thoughts and feelings. Any negative thought in your consciousness must be nipped in the bud. Protect yourself against everything which contributes to the existence of negative thoughts and feelings in your consciousness.

Pay special attention to your children. Do not leave them alone during most of the day. Remember that the fruit which you will get literally in a few years will depend on the direction you show them at the very beginning of their lives and on the knowledge of the laws of this universe which you give them, for your children will grow up and will be able to take responsibilities upon themselves and to serve to the benefit of the earthly evolutions. Each of you is responsible for the future of this planet and for the unfolding of the events in the coming months.

Remember that the tension which was relieved with the cataclysm in the south of Asia at the end of last year is increasing again. As a matter of fact, with your every negative action, every negative thought and feeling you untiringly draw a new cataclysm nearer.

Try to keep the state of inner peace and harmony during most of the day. Do not forget that other people live next to you. If you live in a big city, during the day your aura comes into contact with the auras of thousands of people. When you manage to keep a harmonious state within yourself, you literally infect with this state thousands of people with whose auras you come into contact during the day.

Exactly the same effect occurs when you meet a person looking like a thundercloud and seeking somebody to ease his tension and to vent his anger. But in this case you are infected with the negative energies of this person.

Protect your inner world against the intrusion of negative energies. Take special care about your children.

You may say that nothing depends on you and that your government is to be blamed for everything, because it does not take proper care about you and does not allow you to enjoy a worthy way of life.

Allow me to disagree with you. All things in this world are drawn to each other by their vibrations, and you have exactly that government which can exist only because the majority of the population considers it possible to tolerate this government and its policy.

You constantly exchange energies with thousands of people and thus you constantly exchange karma with them. How do you think, what are the manifestations of a family karma, town karma, country karma or planet karma? Imagine a person who has completely freed himself from his personal karma. What do you think will happen to this person next? Will he ascend?

It is quite probable that such a person can ascend. But let me assure you that a person who has become free from his personal karma acquires an absolutely different expanded consciousness. He rises up to another, higher level of consciousness and understands that it is impossible to save only his own soul. Actually, all is God, and at this new level of consciousness the person feels the unity of all the living much more deeply. Such a person is most likely to stay in embodiment irrespective of whether his external consciousness is aware of his decision or not. He continues to live in the world of his choice. Every day he draws the negative energies of the people around him into his aura and transmutes these energies. Such a person is like a sponge. As soon as he comes in touch with the people's auras saturated with too a big quantity of negative energies, he takes a part of this energy upon himself and neutralises it. A phenomenon occurs which you call the transmutation of the karma of a town, a country or a planet.

Therefore, very much depends on each of you, beloved, on your ability to keep harmony and balance, in spite of any surrounding circumstances. And if you feel depression, lack of joy, causeless melancholy, it means that you have most likely come under the influence of a big mass of negative energy. You have loaded your aura so heavily that you will need some time to be alone or in nature so as to restore your inner peace and balance.

Try to identify your inner state and the reasons of disharmony in your consciousness.

When you reach a certain level of consciousness at which you are allowed to take upon yourself the karma of a town, a country or the planet and to transmute this karma, you serve during 24 hours a day.

This is a vital service, beloved. Today I have given these recommendations in the hope of explaining the technique of such a service to those of you who are already providing this vital service to the world. And now, when you are already aware of your serving, you will be able to take measures for the restoration of your vibrations and energies in good time. Listen keenly to your organism. And, when you are overcome with depression, find a way to build up your inner harmony and peace. For some of you it can be a meditation, for others it can be a prayer, a stroll in nature, listening to relaxing music or playing with children.

Do not allow yourself to be in the negative state of consciousness for a long time. Suppress all the negative vibrations within you as soon as they arise. Do not let them take hold of your being from top to bottom. And remember that you always have an opportunity to appeal to the Ascended Hosts for help as a last resort. We will render to our devoted servants all the help which the Cosmic Law will allow us.

I AM Kuthumi, your brother

A teaching on the karma of poverty and wealth

Lord Surya, May 26, 2005

I AM Surya, having come again from the Great Central Sun to meet you through this messenger. I HAVE come to inform you about an important Teaching on karma and its transmutation.

If you look at the Earth from the viewpoint of the Great Beings of Light dwelling in the eternity, you will see that the entire planet and everything that surrounds you, as well as your four lower bodies, represent nothing else but karma. The Divine Energy spent by the embodied humans who are subject to the living in the lower dense planes of this universe during the current cosmic cycle, while passing through the consciousness of these embodied individuals and being refracted by it, becomes denser and creates the material world around you.

This world gradually manifests itself from the non-manifested state and creates a gigantic stage for you. You come to this stage from embodiment to embodiment to play your parts.

Therefore, in this respect one may say that the entire world around you represents karma or the hardened energy of your wrong actions, thoughts and feelings.

However, even from the experience which you have had in your current life you can understand that it will be scarcely possible to learn something if you actually do not do anything in your life. While being in the embodiment, you learn consistently and you constantly gain life experience. It is impossible for you not to do that, as you are in the material world exactly in order to go through training and to gain the necessary experience.

When your consciousness reaches the required level, it will help you to control the state of the world around you. You will be able to transform the surrounding world by filtering the Divine Energy through your being. As long as your consciousness has a high enough level, your vibrations will be sufficiently high as well. By laying your vibrations on the surrounding world you will be able to transform the physical world and to approximate it to the Divine pattern more and more.

A gigantic Leela[3] is buried here – in this game of the Lord. Being present in each of you, the Lord first creates an illusion and then contracts it. It can be compared to a child, who erects a sand castle, then destroys it and builds another, a more perfect one. With each attempt his creation becomes more perfect and more approximate to the perfection, and every time it surpasses the former creation by its perfection.

You are like gods, and similar to gods you have an opportunity to create and to make perfect images in your life.

Some individuals prefer to follow their own path, they organise their life and the surrounding reality according to the standards which are far from perfection. God allows you to experiment. Sooner or later you will be able to make certain of what in your creation is beautiful and harmonious and keeps within

---

[3] **Leela** or **Lila** is a concept within Hinduism literally meaning "pastime", "sport" or "play". It is common to both monistic and dualistic philosophical schools, but has an obviously different significance in each. Within monism, Lila is a way of describing all reality, including the cosmos, as the outcome of creative play by the divine absolute (Brahman). In the dualistic schools, Lila refers to the activities of God and his devotees, as distinct from the common activities of karma. (translator's footnote)

perfect standards, and what is despicable and ugly and must be transformed.

Therefore, if you prefer to be guided in your life by low standards and non-divine guidelines, you are allowed to do that.

You are in your world only to learn to make a distinction between the Divine patterns and their ugly imitations. You should learn to make a distinction in any sphere of your life. Under the conditions of the dual world everything seems to be dual, so what seems to be good at first sight may appear to be evil, but what seems to be evil may render invaluable help for the evolution of your soul.

That is why it is recommended never to judge with your carnal mind. The worst beggar (according to the standards of your consciousness) may appear to be a spiritually rich man, possessing truly invaluable treasures of his causal body. This individual has come into embodiment intentionally so as to get an experience of a beggarly existence, because his former royal embodiments in the past have not allowed him to gain such experience. To accept a beggarly existence and to surrender to it inside your consciousness is a very high spiritual achievement. Having come into embodiment, many highly evolved souls realised the worth of such experience and decided to give up their property and social status and to become beggars of their own free will. You may know many examples from the written history. I will mention only Francis of Assisi and Gautama Buddha. If you happened to meet Gautama, sitting in the wood during his period of trials, you would probably think him to be some insignificant beggar, unworthy of your attention. And you would make a mistake and miss a chance to have a personal contact with the greatest and ancient spirit.

That is why the gift of making distinctions is so necessary for you.

There is another example. You know that some people have great riches. But do you know that for many of these people their riches are their greatest trial? Do you know how hard it is for them to bear the burden of their riches? I can assure you that among both very rich and very poor people there are highly evolved souls and there are souls who for a long period of time have been turning aside the Divine Path predestined for each soul. The contrasts of your world and the abyss separating the rich and the poor are evidence of the unbalanced karma of your world. At the same time this creates very good conditions for the evolution of your souls.

Yes, beloved, your karma – though this statement may seem strange to you – creates very good conditions for the development of your souls. Your karma is a kind of a coach for you, who constantly puts new pressures on you and does not permit you to relax. Thus, you are constantly in good shape and you are ready to overcome yourself relentlessly and to develop the Divine qualities in yourself.

Both great riches and severe poverty are the consequence of a big karma. But there are cases when a person makes this karma himself, and there are cases when an individual takes this karma upon himself voluntarily in order to work it off in this embodiment and in that way to make the karma of humanity less burdensome.

It is necessary to make distinctions. The most reasonable attitude to richness and poverty should be an equally even and cool attitude both to richness and destitution.

The basic thing is the state of your mind. If you accept both poverty and richness similarly, this is evidence of your nonattachment to the external manifestations. You must develop in yourself a quality of a neutral attitude to the people around you. Neither wealth nor misery is evidence of the evolution of the soul. It is your attitude to the richness and misery that is evidence of the level of your spiritual achievements. When the majority of humans in their consciousness treat correctly the matter of wealth and misery, this will indicate that mankind has worked off this kind of world karma. And there will be neither poor nor rich on earth any longer.

Therefore, truth to tell, the wealth of some people and the poverty of others are just one of the consequences of your imperfect consciousness. Having overcome this imperfection within your consciousness, you will no longer encounter either inordinate poverty or excessive richness in your life.

Thus, your fight both with the rich and the poor makes no sense. It is your fight with your imperfect consciousness which denies poverty and aspires to richness that makes sense. There will be neither poor nor rich people when the consciousness of the majority of humans develops a correct attitude to richness and poverty.

The root of your poverty and of your wealth is the karma of your excessive attachment to the things of this world. You can either voluntarily take this karma upon yourself to work it off or you can make this karma by your incorrect use of the Divine Energy in your previous embodiments.

Everything around you is the consequence of your karma and the karma of humanity – any quality, any manifestation of this world, any feeling and any thought. But all this creates that background and that stage which allow your soul to pass through the most qualitative training and to evolve.

Your life may seem absolutely irreparable to you. But it can probably be a great consolation for you if I say that many Beings of Light envy you, for you have such good conditions for the evolution of your souls. Many of them would gladly change their abode for yours if it were allowed by the Divine Law. Thus, your task is to develop a broader view on the evolution of your souls and, on the whole, on the evolution of the entire mankind and the entire universe.

I will be glad if my talk today contributes to the alteration of your consciousness in the right direction.

I AM Surya, and I am sending you my regards from the Great Central Sun

A teaching on karma

Beloved Kuthumi, May 31, 2005

I AM Kuthumi, having come to you through this messenger again. I HAVE come to give you a small Teaching and to consolidate the knowledge which has already been given in the previous dictations. The Hosts of Light are invisibly present among you. They try to make use of every chance to be present in your world - as soon as a gap in the pure vibrations appcars and allows us to do this.

Our worlds enrich each other reciprocally. Do not think of your world as about the devil incarnate.

Yes, the situation in your world is rather sad today. But this will not last forever. Both the purification of your world and the rise of the vibrations of the physical plane following after it are necessary conditions for the further evolutionary progress of humanity.

Your karma is very large and it consists of the karma both of each individual and the entire planet. This hardened karma - which is in fact condensed energy - creates your dense world.

When the karma is worked off through the rise of the human consciousness, the refusal of the wrong actions and the maintaining of the right Divine accord of thoughts and feelings, the physical plane gradually becomes less and less dense until it disappears altogether. Nevertheless, still long before the physical plane of planet Earth disappears, the life will move from this plane to the higher ones. These planes are brought pretty close to you at present, especially the astral and the mental planes. You can sit inertly at home or even at work, while at the same time your mental or emotional body can wander around the mental and the astral planes. These wanderings can even reach your external consciousness and either be realised by your outer mind or not.

You leave your body and have a journey to the astral plane every night. Your external consciousness does not always realise where you were travelling and whom you met at night. There are individuals capable of remembering their dreams and even of making conscious journeys in their dream in order to meet those people whom they want to meet. Such an activity, as well as any other activity typical of your world, may be used both for good and for evil aims. Everything depends on the aim of the person making astral journeys and the on the motives he is guided by - whether he wishes to influence the individuals whom he meets for his mercenary aims or he does this for the benefit of the planet.

The journeys out of the body in your less dense bodies are quite natural. These journeys take place independently from whether you realise it with your outer consciousness or not.

Nonetheless, I must warn you that if you use a conscious journey to the astral plane in order to influence some person or even to harm him, your actions entail the same karma as if you performed them in the physical plane with full consciousness in broad daylight.

If your external consciousness does not understand what you are doing in the astral plane, this will not free you from the karmic responsibility for your actions as well.

I will tell you more. A lot of individuals create much more karma in their dream than during the vigilant state of their consciousness. In exactly the same way when you are at home and make an unconscious journey to the astral or mental plane while your thoughts and feelings are aimed against any person, you create karma.

If you play mental images of some vindictive or sexual scenes through your consciousness, you create the same karma as if you really performed all these actions in the physical plane. That is why we are never tired of saying to you again and again that you must constantly control your thoughts and feelings. During your night sleep you are drawn to those layers of the astral plane, the vibrations of which in their quality correspond to the quality of your thoughts before the sleep. If before going to bed you watched a horror film or spent time in drunken company, you will be drawn to those layers of the astral plane where you will continue your evening entertainment. In this case you create the same karma as if you were doing all this in the physical plane.

That is why your mood during the day and especially before going to bed is very important. The best thing is to pray or, if you are not used to praying before sleep, at least to listen to soft music or to have a stroll in nature. It would also be useful to read a good kind fairy tale to your children before sleep. And, of course, do not forget before going to bed to ask the angels to accompany you to the etheric octaves of Light where the sacred retreats of the Brotherhood are located.

You can even specify precisely whomever of the Masters you would like to meet during your night's sleep and frame a question, the answer to which you would like to get.

If you ask me a concrete question before sleep, the first thing you should do in the morning is to concentrate and to call to mind the answer given by me during your sleep. As a rule, I give answers to everyone who reaches me in my retreat and asks me questions during his night sleep. It depends only on you to recall this answer and to write it down immediately after awakening.

You see how differently you may spend time during your night sleep. And it is up to you to make a choice as to how to use your night sleep. You literally programme yourselves before sleep for the actions which you perform during your night sleep.

Therefore, I repeat again and again: you must control your thoughts and feelings constantly, every minute. Always remember - if the situations which you bottle up in your mind are subject to the karmic punishment, you create karma by just thinking about them.

In this case the technique of the karma creation is the following. The Divine Energy entering your four lower bodies from the Divine world along the crystal string is tinted by your thoughts and feelings. If your thoughts are imperfect - you qualify the Divine Energy falsely.

It is very important to control the state of your consciousness at every moment. Your consciousness is so mobile that we never cease to marvel at your ability to create so much karma even during your prayers. That is why you are told about the meditation practice as one of the possible ways of soothing your mind.

Only in the case when you manage to calm all your fussy thoughts and feelings and reach a total peace of your mind can you ascend to the higher etheric octaves of Light and stay there for a long time. You become able to meet with the Masters, to talk to them and to stroll with them around the etheric octaves of Light.

For that reason, to be able to judge indirectly the level of your spiritual merits, wind up the alarm-clock so that it can give you a signal every hour. When you hear a signal, try to recall what you were thinking about at that moment. If at that time you were thinking about some elevated and spiritual things, you can mark it as figure "1" on a slip of paper or in your memory. If your thoughts were imperfect, mark it as "0".

It is enough to catch your thoughts ten times a day according to this technique. Sum up all figures "1", append "0" to them and you will see the approximatc percentage of the karma worked off by you. For example, if six out of ten your thoughts could be characterised as elevated, the percentage of the worked off karma is approximately 60%.

It is not strange if one day you fix 10% of the worked-off karma and the next day the result is 70%. In reality your karma changes during the day. The karma is energy. If you spend most of the day in nature and do not communicate with anybody, the percentage of the worked-off karma will be the most approximate to your natural index, achieved by you at a given stage of your development. If you come into contact with thousands of people during the day, you exchange energy with them every time you touch their auras or during conversations and teamwork. Consequently, you exchange karma every time you come into contact with people during the day.

That is why all the venerable old men, prophets and yogis preferred a secluded way of life and did not associate with people. Thus, it is impossible for you not to bear the karma of your family, your town and your planet while you live on earth.

The humans of earth are very interrelated by their karma. In order to become independent from the karma of the people around you it is necessary for you to reach a high level of spiritual achievements.

And do not forget that the Law of Likeness acts in your world. You are drawn exactly to those people and situations to which you are to be drawn in order to work off your karma.

When a Buddha walks on earth, no karmic situation can affect him. He steps on earth without being noticed by anybody and no negative energies can cling to him. However, in order for a Buddha to come to your world, he must first take imperfection or karma upon himself. It is like a diver who takes a stone in his hands before making a dive.

For that reason, you are highly recommended not to judge anyone. You never can say whether it is a Buddha or the lowest sinner standing in front of you, because both of them can be burdened with similar karma at times. But if one of them takes upon himself the karma of humanity intentionally, feeling compassion for people and wishing to help them, the other burdens himself with this karma only owing to his ignorance.

Today I have touched upon some of the topics which were already known to you. We have viewed many questions together from a new angle. The questions of karma are very sophisticated. I raise my hat to the members of the Karmic Board, as I realise how considerable are the difficulties which they encounter in their work.

I AM Kuthumi

A teaching on good karma

Beloved Kuthumi, June 6, 2005

I AM Kuthumi, having come to you again. The purpose of my coming today is to acquaint you with one more viewpoint on the structure of the world. When contacting our reality your sensations do not always reflect the real state of affairs. You are used to grounding your perception of the world according to your sensory organs, and you completely trust your sensory organs. And, really, why in the world should you believe in something you do not see and why should you act in accordance with our recommendations when you do not even have an opportunity to meet with us directly without the help of this messenger?

However, this is a question of your faith. You either believe that the world around you is not the entire Creation and that the entire Creation is actually much larger, or you do not believe it.

You cannot start knowing something which you do not believe in. You cannot sense the things which you know could not exist. However, as soon as you begin to believe in the real world of God which is invisible and not inconceivable for your sensory organs but is not less real because of that, you almost immediately start conceptualising our world.

The subtle worlds contact you and you are constantly coming into contact with the subtle worlds. You just do not pay attention to our reality. But our communication with each of you is not only possible - it is in progress all the time. And the same way as you do not notice radio waves penetrating you constantly, the vibrations of our world come into contact with you all the time and you do not perceive them. But if you properly prepare your temple and - above all - believe in the realness of our world, you will be able to perceive our world inevitably.

Imagine that I have an opportunity to talk to you. I come to you and sit knee to knee with you. You do not see me. You do not see me for two reasons. The first reason is that you do not expect me to come and within your consciousness you are not ready for my arrival. The second reason is that you do not perceive my presence with your physical sensory organs.

Which of the two reasons separating us is the most essential and difficult to surmount? I will tell you that it is the first one. When your consciousness is ready to contact the subtle world and to communicate with the Ascended Hosts, you will start your communication irrespective of whether your sensory organs perceive it or not.

Your organism has untapped, dormant abilities, which enable you to hear without listening, to see without looking, to know and to get information almost immediately without the help of thoughts and words and without the help of your physical perceptive apparatus.

This seems to be fantastic to you. But if you turn to the history of the greatest inventions and discoveries, you will come across an amazing regularity. All these inventions and discoveries burst upon the mind of their inventors out of nowhere. A person would tune in to a certain wave of his thoughts connected with some branch of human activity, and suddenly receive enlightenment in the form of knowledge which appeared in his head out of nowhere.

Certainly, it is very difficult to give any idea of the basic nature of an invention in such a field of the modern knowledge as, for example, the Internet or the contemporary means of communication to a man who has no knowledge in the field of computer programming. But for a person who has knowledge it will not be difficult to receive the new information coming to his external consciousness and connected with the object of his activity. A lot of things like that take place completely spontaneously. And a person who has found out about an invention usually does not even think about the mechanism of its crossing his mind.

The same may be said about you. Having an idea of the Ascended Hosts you can receive information from us which suddenly appears in your head and, even without knowing how it happens, you will be able to be guided by this information in your activity.

If you think carefully, each of you will certainly recollect a few examples of how miraculously you managed to find some lost things or to get an idea of how to behave in a difficult situation or to obtain an utterly miraculous solution to an intricate task in life that you were facing. All these miracles are the interference of the higher plane into your life. And you find the realisation of these lucky chances due to either your Higher Self or the interference of the Ascended Hosts.

The complexity is in the fact that the time passes differently in our worlds. That is why the moment of your request may not coincide with the moment of your receiving the thing requested. It is natural that your requests can be satisfied only if you possess enough good karma for the realisation of your requests.

It seems senseless for a practical man to waste efforts on doing some good things absolutely disinterestedly without a backward glance and without looking forward to getting a reward for his good deed in the near future. But the reason for your seesawing and unwillingness to perform good deeds selflessly is again your disbelief in the Divine Law.

You suppose that if you subscribe to a church, to an orphanage or to some charity organisation, you must immediately receive from God the growth of the money you spend for charity.

But, beloved, everything depends on the basis of your decision to subscribe. If you subscribe with a precondition to receive something in return or if you think that God will forget about the sin you committed, or you subscribe in order to show everybody your generosity, this sacrifice will not create good karma for you. You must just perform good deeds without thinking about the consequences and the advantages which this sacrifice can bring you in the future.

In this case you really create good karma. And this good karma of yours can help you when you are in a difficult situation and call to God and ask Him for help. God will lend you a hand. It is impossible for God not to help you. But for this help exactly that energy of your causal body will be used which makes your good karma.

And if you do not have enough good karma at the moment of your request, you will not receive the help you need and ask for.

You receive exactly what you give to the world. And if you have not performed at least one good deed during all your life and during all your previous lives, then why do you think God will respond to your request when you are in need?

For that reason, if I were you in embodiment, I would funnel all my energies and put up all my cash assets into succouring those living beings who need my help. In this case your good deeds will accumulate in the form of energy in your causal body. It is like when you save money for a rainy day. The difference is only in that you save your money in the form of energy in another world. But there is no more reliable place in your world for keeping this energy and your savings. This energy of yours can be always requested by you through your appeal to God at a moment when you need Divine help.

Consequently, when you call to God and say, "Help me, oh Lord!" and if at that moment there is not enough energy in your depository in Heaven to help you, do not hold it as a grievance against God, hold it as a grievance against yourself, because this is you who have not cared about yourself and have not stocked the necessary amount of good karma in order to create a reserve of your merits in Heaven.

Today I have given you a very important Teaching on good karma. I hope that you will be able to reduce this Teaching to practice. Just picture how it could be good for you if you took this Teaching as a guideline in your life and how it would be great if all people on earth made a dash for creating good karma. Each of you would be able to receive all the necessary help from the people who would literally be run off their feet around earth in search of those who are in need of their help. Besides, if you created the necessary amount of good karma, you could always appeal to God for help and receive help.

I wish you to succeed in your practice of creating good karma. May you create only good karma henceforward and for the rest of your life.

I AM Kuthumi

A teaching on the serpent-tempter and the serpent of wisdom

Lord Maitreya, June 17, 2005

I AM Maitreya, having come to you.

The delightful moment of our communication has come. And I have come to share my knowledge and thoughts with you.

It is always possible to find Divine manifestations in everything surrounding you in your world. And it is always possible to find the things that are not from God. There are many more things not from God in your world so far. Your world does not belong to the Divine worlds. Very long ago your world was not material and its vibrations were close to the Divine vibrations. That was millions of years ago. Man did not have a physical body. Everything around him was like a garden in paradise. Man lived like a plant. The consciousness of man was irreproachable. And everything was fine except for one little thing. Man did not have mind. But since man did not have mind, he was not able to create. He could not create and he could not evolve. The existence of man was like that of animals.

The Higher Cosmic Forces were no longer able to maintain the existence of man who had no mind and, consequently, had no chances for his development. Therefore, the Sons of the Sun, the Sons of Wisdom descended into the bodies of the humans and endowed them with the opportunity to obtain mind – the fire of mind, with the help of which man acquired an ability to create like Gods.

I am giving you this legend in an uncomplicated way for your present level of consciousness in order to help you to comprehend your own history best – and exactly to understand the moment of the beginning of your fall into the matter. As man was gradually becoming able to use his mental faculties, he obtained an ability to choose where to direct the energy flowing into his bodies from the Divine Source.

You know the legend about Adam and Eve. You are aware of the serpent that tempted Eve. But you think it was someone outside you. In fact, so it was. Man got his mind from outside of himself. The Masters of Wisdom, the Masters of Mind descended into the bodies of people to endow the latter with mind. Man had been an irrational being before that event. But after that event man became conscious of self. He began to make choices consciously. And exactly after having been endowed with mind man started to create karma.

Plants do not have karma; animals do not have karma either. Karma, as a consequence of an action, is inherent only in the creatures that possess mind. Therefore, as soon as man had acquired mind, he became responsible for his actions – for everything he was doing on earth.

Thus, the human mind became man's greatest delight and his greatest misfortune at the same time.

Man has always suspected intuitively that someone outside him was responsible for everything happening to him. This is both right and wrong, because after man had acquired mind it became an integral part of him. And he could no longer blame anyone for the things that happened to him. Man was creating karma by using the Divine energy in a way which did not correspond to the Divine plan. The Divine energy was assuming density and formed the world which surrounded man. In this way the material world was being created and the karma was being made.

Man can blame the outer forces, Lucifer and the fallen angels for all the disasters that have happened to him. You can find other names in other legends.

However, if man had not received mind, he would not have been able to be in line with the idea God had designed while creating him. We were even confronted with the question of the abolishment of the earthly evolution as not corresponding to the Divine plan.

For that reason, it is not logical to blame those who gave you a chance to continue your evolution for all your sins. In reality after a human had been endowed with a spark of mind the karma of his wrong actions started to fall upon both this human and the Master who had sacrificed his particle to him. As a result, everything has been intertwined and can be untangled only after man has had his share of pleasure in the illusion created by him and is able to realise the Higher Path which exists and is predetermined for him.

The human mind is the greatest punishment and at the same time a good opportunity for man to go through the physical world like going through purgatory, to be purged from what is non-divine and to become the one he must become in the end – a God-man.

The key to your evolution is inside your consciousness. And unless and until you seek those outside you who are guilty in your troubles and misfortunes, you will occupy a position which does not lead you to the positive changes. You can reason very long upon whom is to be blamed for the recent hurricane which swept away hundreds of thousands of human lives. But until you set to work with good will and start hurricane response management nothing will change.

Thus, the main thing for you now is to understand that your standpoint of looking for the guilty outside you is not an affirmative approach. You must understand that nobody but you is responsible for everything that happens in your life. And having understood this you should begin to solve the tangle of all the karma you have created during hundreds and thousands of embodiments. You work off your karma every second of your stay on earth when you overcome an outer situation within your consciousness and come up with a right inner attitude to everything happening around you.

Therefore, the sooner you stop seeking the guilty outside you, the sooner you will be able to overcome the limits of space and time which you have created for yourselves.

The Earth is like a huge ant-hill. And every single individual on earth is connected with every living creature on the planet. Our task is like that of the sun which clothes your ant-hill with light and sends you its vivifying rays. And these rays make you wake up, stretch your limbs which are asleep after the night, move and perform the work you should perform.

And your absolutely unique instrument which you have been polishing during the period of your evolution on planet Earth is turning from your punishment into your blessing, because it is exactly owing to your mind that you can ascend to the greatest peaks of the Divine consciousness that are inapproachable without the absolutely unique experience you have gained during the period of your embodiments on planet Earth.

Your mind is the very thing to have cast you into the whirlpool of materiality and your mind is the very thing to help you get out of this whirlpool of materiality. And the Divine qualities of your mind which you have obtained during the period of your wandering in the material world will remain and transit together with you to the other, Higher World. But you yourselves must give up the lower qualities of your mind represented by your carnal mind.

That is why your task is to learn to distinguish in yourselves everything that is from God from the things of this world that you have created yourselves. Your physical world is like your parental nest where you feel comfy. But sooner or later the moment comes for you to leave your nest since you have grown up and become ready to spread your wings and fly.

May every dogma which has found lodgement in your consciousness be overcome. Every nestling in order to hatch must break through the shell with its own strength. Therefore, your urgent task is to make every effort in order to break through the boundaries of the dogmas and to acquire an ability to look unbiased at any legend.

Your wits, your mind is the very serpent-tempter that enticed you from the path of virtue and it was your choice to pass the peccant path on planet Earth. At the same time your mind is the serpent of wisdom that will set you on the Path of righteousness and help you to choose the Higher Path.

Just think whether the time has come for you and whether it is high time to exert every effort to break through the shell of the dogmas and ignorance. Think over the dual meaning of the symbol of serpenthood hidden both in the serpent-tempter and the serpent of wisdom.

You have been descending, but the time has come for you to start your ascension.

I AM Maitreya, your Guru

About the opportunity to unburden your karma of the next month and about the letters to the Karmic Board

Beloved Surya, June 23, 2005

I AM Surya, having come to you today through my messenger.

Today is such a day when you can put in your devotional efforts and direct the energy of a prayer onto the transmutation of the karma of the next month. Your request will be granted precisely to the extent of the purity and sincerity of your hearts and as much as the Law of karma will allow it.

That is why I recommend you not to be lazy but to work on this day. You can even dedicate all your actions during this day to the transmutation of karma. While washing up and tidying up your apartments just imagine that you are washing away all the karmic layers of the past from everything your hands touch. The water is your helper.

You may expand your experiment and transfer it to the mental plane. You may imagine yourself taking a duster and washing away all the dark thoughts which have ever come into your mind. After that you can move to the astral plane and wash away all the layers of your negative feelings.

Just imagine yourself spring-cleaning all your bodies. You can visualise yourself taking off your mental body or your astral body like clothes and dusting your imperfect thoughts and feelings out of them. The air is your helper. You can place your bodies under the sun and expose them to the rays of the bright summer sun in order for the sun to transmute the traces of your karma. The sun is your helper.

You may visualise the violet flame penetrating all your bodies and burning everything not from God in your four lower bodies. The flame is your helper.

On this day the Karmic Board meeting starts on earth. You may apply to the Karmic Board with your letters and requests. You task is to ask for help. The task of the Karmic Board is to consider your request and to render you the help the cosmic mercy can render you. Ask the angels to deliver your letters to the addressee; do not forget to put your name, last name and the date and burn the letter. If you decide to keep a copy of your letter, you will find out in some time that much, if not all, of your request to the Karmic Board has come true.

The burden of karma hanging over mankind is too heavy, and the Ascended Hosts use literally every chance to help you, the people of earth who are in embodiment now. Do not neglect the mercy and the opportunities granted to you.

The Cosmic Law does not allow us to intervene into your karma if you do not ask us about our intervention. But as soon as an appeal has been pronounced and heard, the Ascended Hosts are ready to render you all the possible help.

However, you should not rely entirely on the Ascended Hosts. If a human asks once for help with getting rid of some heavily-loaded karma, such as the karma of an abortion, we help. But, if some time later this human commits the same action again and creates the same karma, the Ascended Hosts find it much more difficult to help in this case.

Therefore, every time you ask for help in the deliverance of the consequences of your wrong actions in the past, you must consciously take upon yourself the duty never to repeat in your life such actions which lead to the creation of karma. And if it is difficult for you to constantly bear in mind your obligation not to create karma, take a clean sheet of paper and list the qualities in you that you think are negative and that you want to get rid of. Every time you start your devotional ritual, direct the energy of a prayer onto the dissolution of the energies contained in your four lower bodies that are burdening them greatly due to the heavy errors committed by you in the past.

If the knowledge of the Law of karma or the Law of retribution were widespread among the people of earth and especially among the youth, it would be possible to prevent many actions of humans committed by them due to their ignorance.

To know the Law of karma is the first step necessary for every individual in order not to sin but to act in life according to the Divine principles.

Therefore the major task for each of you in the near future is to acquaint the more people the better with the Law of karma or retribution. And the best example will be your own. Show your example to your child, your family, your colleagues at work.

The negative energy cannot evaporate by itself. But the energy of your prayers can dissolve the negative karma, just as it can be dissolved by your visualisations which I mentioned at the beginning of our meeting today. And the energy of the good karma created by your right actions can be directed at your will onto the unburdening of the karmic loads and on providing you with the easiest path to work off your karma.

You must work off the karma of your wrong actions, but you can do it for example by either falling or having a fracture or by getting off easily with a light bruise or a livid spot. That is why I recommend you to apply with a request to the Karmic Board today or in the near future. You can also specify in your letter what you concretely promise to do in order to direct the energy of your actions onto the unburdening of your karmic loads.

This may be a responsibility to say a certain number of prayers or Rosaries during a definite period of time. This may also be a responsibility to help the penniless and the infirm.

Only such responsibilities should be taken upon yourself that are not beyond your power to fulfil. If you take upon yourself too many responsibilities in the hopes of working off as much karma as possible, you can find yourself unequal to the task. Do not forget that you will have to pass through tests in your life and to maintain the highest state of consciousness in spite of all the barriers and life disturbances you will have to encounter.

The negative vibrations and the irritation you can feel if you fall down on the task taken upon yourself can blot out the positive effect from your right actions and deeds.

Do not understand your task as first to sin and then to repent of the sins. Your task is not to create new karma. Yet, you will have to work off your old karma in one form or another. For that reason, be careful not to create new karma.

Our talk today has been very useful as it has provided you with the tools that, if used correctly, will be the keystone of your success in the progress on the Path. Keep in mind that the unreal part of you, your ego, will look for any chance to set you on the wrong track and to prove to you that your prayers and letters are of no use, that you are exhausted today and can relax without fulfilling the responsibilities undertaken.

You have been creating your karma during millions of years, during your countless earthly embodiments. And do you really wish to get rid of your karma in a moment?

If the Law allowed you to experience the consequences of an instantaneous return of karma, no human would endure for a split second the effect of the negative energy he would be snowed under. You would be literally torn asunder. For that reason, the Law of karma returns your karmic duties for performance to you gradually during a significant period of time. And the help you ask us for cannot be given to you at once either. We need time to render you help. The time for rendering help can be different for each of you depending on the heaviness of the karma, the content of your request and the responsibilities you undertake upon yourself. The time of giving help can also be different and take a period from six months to twelve years.

Consequently, you should gird yourself for everyday labour. Miracles are possible in your life, but you predetermine the miracles in your life yourselves by creating good karma day after day.

I AM Surya

A teaching on the karma of inactivity

Beloved Kuthumi, June 24, 2005

I AM Kuthumi, having come again.

Our talk today will be dedicated to the karma of inactivity. Have you ever heard of the karma of inactivity? It seems to you that only your actions can create karma. In the course of our previous talks you have become familiarised with both the notion of karma[4] and the process of its creation. You have also had a chance to get an insight into good karma[5]. And now I want to return to the topic of karma and to give you a Teaching on the karma of inactivity.

Imagine that someone turns to you for help but you do not wish to help. Will you create karma in this case? You will not do anything, will you? You will not make any effort in order to help the person who asks you for help. A lot of people on earth create karma precisely by doing nothing in situations when they should act.

You see that in Divine Law you create karma even if you are inactive. You come to your world in order to act and to gain experience. Consequently, if you avoid acting, you create karma.

Let me give an explanation of this point. You remember that karma is the energy which you qualify incorrectly by performing wrong actions. If the Divine Energy coming to you from the Divine world is used by you in accordance with the Divine Law, you create good karma – your treasure in Heaven. If you misuse the Divine Energy, it accumulates in your four lower bodies in the shape of negative energy. And in accordance with the Divine Law this energy attracts to

---

[4] "A teaching on karma" *Beloved Kuthumi, May 31, 2005*

[5] "A teaching on good karma" *Beloved Kuthumi, June 6, 2005*

you the situations you have to pass through again and again so as to learn your lesson, to make a right choice and thus to work out your karma. For example, if you envy somebody or take offence at somebody, or you talk behind somebody's back, you create karma. And this karma will return to you most probably in the form of situations when you yourselves will be treated badly in exactly the same way. You will be envied or caused offence to or venomous tongues will talk about you. And in order to work out your karma you will have to pass through all these situations with humility and obedience to the Will of God, without fulminating your insulters, and by being infinitely forgiving to the people who do harm you.

That is why Jesus told that you should forgive "up to seventy times seven".[6] You never know how many times in your past lives you offended people and allowed yourselves to behave abominably towards them.

And now let us return to the karma of inactivity. Imagine that a man asks for your help and you refuse to help him. Will you create karma by acting so? You do not waste the Divine Energy, do you? You just do not do anything. This situation is not as simple as it may seem. And whether you will or will not create karma in this case depends on many conditions.

First of all you must be sure that a person who turns to you for help really needs it. If a person asks for your help and does not need it, but you give him this help anyway, this person creates karma. You do not create karma in this case, but indirectly you help the other person to create karma. When you reach a certain spiritual level, you are obliged not only to attend to

---

[6] *Matthew 18:22*

your affairs, but to help other people avoid situations in which they create karma.

And now comes the next moment. If a person who turns to you for help really needs it, you will not create karma if you refuse this man because you cannot help him.

No doubt a person can get into hot water and really be in urgent need of help e.g. financial help. And he turns to you for help. But if you have no opportunity to help this person or you think you should primarily use your money to feed your family, you do not create karma in this case. It is highly probable that the person who turns to you for help refused to help you in one of the past lives when you were asking him and now you are simply returning his karmic debt to him.

And finally, if a person turns to you for help and really needs it, but you refuse to help him though you can do it, you create karma. You are obliged to help the people who ask you for help. When you can help but refuse to, it seems to you that you are not wasting Divine Energy and, consequently, are not creating karma. However, the senses and motives by which you are guided towards this decision make you create karma. For example, you want to teach this person a lesson, or it is pleasant for you when someone licks your feet, or you cannot be bothered to help somebody, or you are driven by greed. Any of these and many other such character traits, when they are the true reason for your refusal to help, are non-divine and you create karma by manifesting them. Therefore, before you refuse to help a person who asks you for help always weigh all pros and cons thoroughly.

And your sure adviser in a difficult situation is undoubtedly your Higher Self, because your Higher Self always knows whether you should give help or not.

If your connection with your Higher Self is impeded or you are not sure about the answers received, try to analyse your inner motive and feelings thoroughly. You do not want to help this person because you either cannot be bothered or you pinch pennies and grudge the time. Or you start condemning this person for having deteriorated to such a state that he cannot solve his problems himself. If such thoughts creep into your head, try to overcome them, force yourself and render the help you are asked for. And after you have given help you will feel a relief and this will be a sign that you have done the right thing and worked out some old karma of the past.

If you do not feel any negative feelings, but your intuition suggests that you should not help this person in spite of the fact that the person needs help, asks you for it and you are able to help him, that means there could be a one percent chance that you are giving the person who turns to you a test. Yet, tests like this are very rare and you must possess a high spiritual level and go through initiations and be granted the mantle of a Guru in order to have a right to give such tests. Therefore, I recommend that you always help a person who needs help and refers to you for help when you are able to do so.

In reality, a lot of problems in your world are connected exactly with the fact that people ask for help and do not receive it, for example, from officials who are supposed to give help and even receive salary appendant to their position for this purpose, but who do not give the help to the people asking them.

You should always remember that in your next life you will reverse roles and the official who does not perform his duty properly due to his neglect will find himself in a pleading position and will have to appeal for help exactly to those individuals whom he refused to help.

Exactly the same problem will crop up before the high and mighty who are very wealthy. Big money is always evidence that this person's karma is connected with his wrong attitude to money.

Wealth is given to people as a chance to work out such karma. Therefore, a person on whom wealth drops from the clouds to enable him to work out his karma should analyse very attentively how he can dispose of this wealth in order to give help to as many needy people as possible. Yet, he should specifically give help to the destitute but not waste money on theatrical philanthropy. For if a person disposes of his wealth wrongly and wastes it on pleasures or objects of luxury and prestige, it is 99 percent probable that in his next life he will receive the return of his karma and will be born into a very poor family and his portion in life will be begging from-door-to door during all his life, hardly making both ends meet.

Thus, never envy those people who possess big money. Big money is evidence of great karma in the present and, if used wrongly, of a greater karma in the future.

I think our talk has been effective today. At any rate this knowledge can help you avoid the karma of inactivity in your lives.

I AM Kuthumi

About the new Divine dispensation

Beloved El Morya, June 27, 2005

I AM El Morya, having come to you again.

Since the moment of our last meeting an important event has taken place about which I would like to tell you in the course of our conversation today. You know that on the 23rd of each month you are provided with an opportunity to transmute your karma of the following month with the help of reading prayers, decrees, Rosaries or mantras.

You also know that on the 23rd of June the proceedings of the Karmic Board began and it will be in session for two weeks. In the course of this session it was decided that beginning from the next month - the 23rd of July 2005 - and on the 23rd of each month including the 23rd of December this year you will be granted an unparalleled opportunity to transmute your personal karma and the karma of the planet.

Those of you who find time on the 23rd of each month to perform an easy ritual which I will describe below will create conditions for their progress and for the transition to the new level of consciousness. Such an opportunity has never been granted before. You can take advantage of this opportunity only till the end of this year. And you will see how far your consciousness is able to progress in its desire to achieve a higher level. In fact, the only thing which separates you from a higher level of consciousness is your karma. It covers you like a dome, and you are unable to see the things as they are in reality, because you are prevented from doing so by the negative energy contained in your four lower bodies.

If a high enough number of people transmute their karma for at least one hour during the day on the 23rd of each month till the end of this year, the efforts you make on karma transmutation will be multiplied in proportion to the number of people who take part in this devotional vigil.

Thus, for example, if on the 23rd of July, 23rd of August, 23rd of September, 23rd of October, 23rd of November and 23rd of December you devote one hour a day to the transmutation of the karma of the following month and if one thousand people all over the globe take part in this vigil together with you, your efforts will be multiplied thousandfold. If ten thousand people take part in the vigil, your efforts will be intensified myriads of times.

That is why I ask you to take to heart this new opportunity granted to you by God. Do not miss your chance. We are fully aware of the fact that many people reading these dictations belong to different religious confessions and adhere to different devotional practices. So, you should not be embarrassed by the fact that you will not be united by a communal prayer. Read your usual prayers and decrees. The most important thing is the tuning of your consciousness. You should aspire with all your being to join your personal efforts together with the efforts of thousands of lightbearers from all over the world. Just imagine how much Light will be released on these days! And all this Light will be used in accordance with your calls and will be intensified proportionally to the number of people who take part in the vigil on the 23rd of each of the months mentioned above.

If you are not used to the devotional practice, you can find an hour and devote it specially to the ritual described above. In the process of the ritual you can do your everyday chores, for example clean your apartment, work on your grounds or just be at your work place, but you should constantly maintain the highest available level of consciousness and direct the energy which comes to your bodies from the Divine reality at this moment onto the transmutation of the karma of the following month.

Do your usual and habitual work during the day and at the same time constantly try to visualise the energy coming into your heart along the crystal string and to concentrate on directing it onto those situations in your and the planet's life that require transformation.

You may even be unaware of how to solve the problems you face in your life. Just send the Divine energy into such a situation and ask to use this energy for its Divine solution.

If your living circumstances allow it, you can devote more than an hour to this vigil – as much as is not burdensome for you. The Earth needs a spring-clean. Let us direct our efforts together onto this spring-clean until the end of this year.

Remember that the flow of the Divine energy which you will be able to send and which will be multiplied depends on the purity of your motives and hearts. So, if you try to use this dispensation with a mercenary motive or in order to settle old scores, you will create karma which will be also multiplied in proportion with the number of people participating in the vigil. Consequently, if your motive is not pure enough, it would be better for you to refrain from taking part in the vigil.

Such is the peculiarity of your world, unfortunately. And any dispensation, any Divine mercy in your world is something that cuts both ways. Your world is a place where the grain is separated from the weeds. And it is you with your actions who separate within yourselves the things which are from God from those which are not from God. For some people this dispensation will result in an unprecedented growth of their consciousness, while for others the time will come to make a final choice whom to serve.

You do not even need to concentrate on where your energy is directed. The energy will be made the best of. Just express a desire on this day to give your Divine energy for the transmutation of your personal karma, your country's karma or the planet's karma. And the more disinterestedly you sacrifice your energy, the faster and more correctly will all the karmic situations in your life be resolved.

Allow the Supreme Law to use your energy. Do not make it a condition that God should help you to resolve your situation as you think proper. God grants each of you an opportunity to redeem errors. Just wish always to obey the Will of God. Even if you are bedridden or wheelchair-bound due to a disease and can neither read prayers nor work, just send your Love to that Master to whom you feel a special affinity. It can be Mother Mary or Jesus, or Saint Germain. Your Love is the best and the purest energy which will be multiplied without fail.

I would like to stress the fact that each of you has an opportunity to take advantage of this dispensation. Each of you has a chance to rise in his consciousness onto a higher level and to free yourself from a huge part of your karma. But you should endeavour with the best efforts of your heart for that. You should do it sincerely and open-heartedly. It is your own purity and sincerity that determine whether you will receive your reward in the form of ascension onto a new stage of the Divine consciousness at the end of the year. Try not to slip down and not to yield to bad thoughts and motives.

I hope we will be able to meet with you at the end of the year and to add up all the benefits of this new opportunity granted to you.

I AM El Morya, with the Faith in your success

A teaching on karma descending at the end of the year

Beloved Kuthumi, December 19, 2005

I AM Kuthumi, having come to you through our messenger.

I HAVE come to give you a Teaching on how you should regard the karma which descends upon you at the end of the year, what this karma is and how you should treat its descending.

You know that your four lower bodies contain energetic records about the incorrect, abominable and non-divine behaviour which you perpetrated during your present or one of your past lives. These can be records of steady negative conditions which you were experiencing in the past and which you have not been able to get rid of up to this day.

You are aware of the karma which returns to you. You are aware of the karma which is activated within your aura in accordance with the Law of Cosmic Cycles and which crops up before you in the form of some situation, feeling or poor state of your consciousness. This return of karma takes place perpetually and gradually during the whole year. But when the annual cycle is nearly over you come up against a slightly different situation. It might happen that the karma which was returning to you during the year in accordance with the Cosmic Law was not worked off by you as much as the Law requires. And imagine that during this particular one-year cycle other people were also not able to work off their karma by making wise choices, praying or by doing good deeds.

In this case at the end of the year an accumulation of surplus karma takes place. This karma looms over humanity and is ready to make a descent upon it in the form of various states inherent in mankind - diseases, depression, famine or in the form of different calamities and natural catastrophes.

In any case, at the end of the year you can feel even by your subjective sensation that you experience some excessive heaviness. This is just that extra karmic burden which lies on humanity in the shape of non-transmuted negative energy.

That is why it is so important to maintain enforced discipline of your consciousness at the end of the year. In this case it is very helpful for you to consciously lay restrictions upon yourselves, such as fasting, refraining from talk, devotional vigils or help to the poor and destitute which you can offer as a sacrifice to the altar of service.

In so doing you create additional good karma which can be used for the purpose of balancing the situation on the whole planet in the worst extremity.

That is why we keep coming to you during this new cycle of dictations and continually remind you about a probable cataclysm or an act of God. It is not that we want to awe you into praying. No, we come to explain to you the heavy current situation on earth and to offer those of you who are ready to come out as co-creators with God and the Hierarchy of Light that exists in the universe.

If your consciousness is not ready for service of a like nature, it is rather probable that you will mistake our requests for misguided intimidation.

But let us reason upon this together. Is there any alternative? Is there any other way of liquidating the excessive masses of negative energy accumulated on the planet? Do you think there will be some magic and all your energy that you were not able to transform in the particular one-year period will just evaporate by some miracle?

All the miracles of a like nature, even if they did take place in the past, always required a great amount of additional energy. This energy was granted to your planet either from the cosmic reserves or from the causal bodies of the Ascended Masters.

Now picture a company which shows a net loss from year to year. The owner of the company borrows finances from other companies – profitable ones – and covers the loss. And such a state of things can last for some period of time. But there comes a time when the owner realises that the loss is not a stochastic phenomenon but is connected with the neglect of the employees of this company.

So, a good contriver can either make his employees work better or close the company.

And the measures being taken by the Ascended Hosts now are aimed at giving the best representatives of mankind an impetus to work better. You do not want to lose your work place - your planet, using the analogy just cited, do you?

Therefore, it is necessary to have a clear understanding of the alternative the planet is facing at the present moment. You are either able to undertake upon yourselves the responsibility for the situation on the planet, or you will be deprived of the opportunity to continue the evolution on this planet as it will be deemed as a dead-end.

Of course, all this cannot happen in a moment. You will be given a chance to realise your responsibility gradually. In order to make our persuasion more forcible we warned you earlier[7] that we will no longer

---

[7] "Each of your acts of service to all the living creatures reduces the probability of the next threatening cataclysm." *Lord of the World*

stem the flood of karma which is being created by people living in particular localities. And this karma will return literally all at once in the form of one or another technogenic or natural cataclysm.

The probability of such cataclysms increases nearer by the end of the year. That is why you are strongly recommended to undertake more consciously your spiritual practices, prayers and meditations precisely at the end of the year.

There are people whose consciousness is at such a low level that it is useless to speak about such things with them. But, luckily for them, their extent of karmic responsibility is low in comparison with those individuals who realise all the complexity of the situation, but due to their inherent imperfections, laziness and short views do not undertake those actions which we ask them about.

Depending on the level of consciousness reached by people, the Law of Karma operates in different ways. And what can be forgiven for some people is unforgivable for others. You should not care about the fact that somebody's behaviour is improper, but still no karma descends upon him to teach him a lesson.

Purely and simply, this person has either enough time for his evolution or abundant supplies of good karma. Do not worry. The Karmic Law operates faultlessly. And everyone will be given an opportunity to encounter the karma which he created in the past.

Do not think about others, think about yourself. Think about how you personally can mitigate your karma, your family's karma and the karma of your country and planet.

Gautama Buddha, May 2, 2005. The dictation is published in the book "Words of Wisdom", Booksurge, 2008.

You may not have a clear understanding of all the nuances of this universal Law, but you should have a general idea about it and you should tell those who are not yet familiar with this Law of Karma about it. The more people know about this universal Law, the higher is the probability that they will avoid committing unseemly deeds in their lives.

When karma descends upon you, most commonly you are unable to associate the cause-effect relations between your actions and their consequences that descend upon you in the form of different troubles and diseases.

And you exclaim, "For what, Lord?!" instead of accepting with humility everything that God sends you.

Believe me, God is very merciful. And the karma which descends upon you returns to you in the most possible mitigated way.

If you had a chance to understand which of your actions burden you with this or that karmic responsibility you would thank God for allowing you so mercifully to work off what you yourselves committed in the past.

There are several ways of working off your karma.

The first way is not to create karma at all.

The second way is to work off your karma by making right choices.

The third way is to work off your karma by accepting with humility any situation into which you get.

And, finally, you can mitigate your karmic burden by praying and true repentance.

This is what we request you to do strenuously during the period remaining till the end of this year.

Now you have an opportunity to realise that everything that the Masters ask you about is justified and expedient.

None of us has an intention of awing you into doing something.

We speak to you as to sensible people who are standing just slightly lower on the steps of the evolutionary ladder.

I AM Kuthumi. And I was happy to share crumbs of my knowledge with you

Faith is the remedy that you need

Beloved El Morya, December 21, 2005

I AM El Morya Khan, having come to you through my messenger.

I HAVE come to bring to your attention a vital offer which I am empowered to make this afternoon.

Just as during the previous cycle of dictations, I am now very determined. And if any of you doubt my determination and the gravity of my intentions, it is better for you not to read our messages, because you create in your consciousness a formidable barrier and block not only the stream of the Divine Truth, but of the Divine Energy as well.

Your consciousness belongs to your dual world, therefore only those things can happen in your world which you admit within your consciousness. For that reason we will never tell you until the end of the chapter what kind of catastrophe you are probably facing, irrespective of the complexity of the situation on the planet. That is because if you only conceive the idea of a forthcoming catastrophe in your consciousness, this idea will be multiplied, and instead of extinguishing the fire you will rekindle it over and over again.

That is why we will never tell you the copious information which we possess. But we will never become tired of warning and asking you to do all your best in order to harmonise the situation on the planet.

You have noticed that from the moment of the beginning of the new cycle of dictations through our messenger there was no one joyful and optimistic among them. That is not because some changes have taken place within our messenger and she has been intimidated by the sinister cataclysms. All is well with our messenger. And I can assure you that our messages are transmitted with a very high degree of reliability. No, the matter is in the fact that we actually deal with a situation of strain. And with the best will in the world we still cannot implant aspirations in your mind to take upon yourselves those responsibilities which we are asking you about. The law of free will which is operating in your physical octave does not allow us to intervene and to force you. For that reason we can only ask you or, as a last resort, demand of you. But the only thing that will make you act, it seems, is the threatening circumstance which we are talking about.

Well, you seem to prefer acting in accordance with the Russian proverb, "One believes in wonder when hears a sound of thunder".

There are so few people who seriously perceive our information and who are ready to sacrifice much in order to comply with our requests.

Yet, we cannot manage to enlarge the circle of people capable of concrete actions. However, think over the fact that no matter how clearly and duly we reiterate our warnings you are still unable to answer our call.

The matter is not even in your laziness and neglect. The whole point is in the fact that you are so captured by the illusion that you can differentiate neither the source containing the Truth nor the vibrations characteristic of the true source.

Therefore, all your practices and all your actions should be directed on mastering the ability of making distinctions. In reality your sojourn in the illusion will come to an end only when you learn how to make a distinction between the events which take place in the illusive plane and the events belonging to the real Divine world. And your task is to acquire a distinct vision and to learn to make a cold evaluation of every event and fact which you face in life.

It seems to you that your life runs smoothly, and at times you do not even guess that in this silence and smooth tide of life there are hidden agendas, capable of upsetting the peaceful tide of your life in a moment. Therefore, try to withstand this somnolent tranquillity. You are getting your lessons continually. And sometimes one small stone lying on the rails is enough to make your huge train of life leave the track at great speed and turn over. However, you yourselves prepare your own future by making your everyday choices.

When the critical mass of your wrong choices reaches the limits of permissible karma you encounter those situations in your life which literally destroy everything you are used to, and you exclaim in surprise:"Oh, Lord, what have I done wrong? For what has it all fallen to my lot?"

It is a well-known picture, isn't it? And the next step of 90 per cent of people will be to curse God and the Masters for what happened in their lives. They blame all the people around them and the whole world instead of accepting humbly all that happened to them as a punishment or as a karmic retribution which boiled over the permissible limits and returned to them in the form of a horrible judgment.

Thus, on the one hand, in the course of the entire period of existence mankind has been warned and preached to. On the other hand, only when something terrible happened to people were they able to think for a short time about the reasons for the things which fell upon them.

And no matter how much we speak and give you the best counsels in order to avoid the things apprehended, you are not able to believe that everything you are told about is true. And the reason for your disobedience and short-sightedness is the lack of the true Faith.

That is why I, the Master who represents the aspect of God's Will, address you this afternoon. And I can help each of you who will turn to me with a request to enhance his Faith.

Faith is the remedy that you need. And I am speaking now not about an implicit faith based on ignorance and intimidation. I am referring to the Faith based on the exact knowledge of the Law which exists in this universe.

And this Law is the Law of causal relationship, or the Law of Karma, or retribution. This Law operates regardless of whether you want it to or not and independently of your will. This is what is real. And that is on what your aspiration to assert your free will regardless of any circumstances stubs its toe. And if this natural barrier provided by the Creator did not stand on the path of your misuse of free will, the question of existence of not only your planet but of the universe itself would be brought into challenge.

For that reason, the first thing you should accept within yourselves is the supremacy of Law governing in this universe and in your lives.

You can appeal to me with a request to enhance your Faith. And I will gladly provide you with this aid as it is the most vital and immediate relief that you need.

I AM El Morya Khan, with the faith in your victory!

On the letters to the Karmic Board

Gautama Buddha, December 22, 2005

I AM Gautama Buddha, having come to you through our messenger again. I HAVE come to you at this dark time of the year when the whole northern hemisphere, where the basic mass of the population of the Earth is concentrated, has very little sun energy at its disposal. It is truly a dark time of the year. And you can feel by your health that even the approaching holidays do not facilitate you to keep up.

I have come to you to give one more message, at the heart of which there is our concern about the planet and about the very existence of life on this planet.

However hard the Ascended Hosts were trying during the past year they did not succeed in achieving the balance on the planet which is necessary for its steady progression. In a state of awareness and with great attention we are anticipating the decision to be announced after the session of the Karmic Board which is now beginning. You know that at this dark time of the year an annual session of the Karmic Board begins. At this session vital decisions are adopted, according to which the planet will be living during the following six months till the next session of the Karmic Board which takes place in the period of the summer solstice.

And so, you can also take part in this session of the Karmic Board and thus influence the course of the planet's progress during the next half-year. Of course, you will not be allowed to enter the hall of the session of the Karmic Board. You will not be able to be present there either in your physical or in your higher bodies. But you can appeal to the Karmic Board with your letters. And I assure you that each of your letters will be thoroughly considered.

There are times when one letter written by a fervent soul is enough to change a decision of the Karmic Board. That is why I highly recommend you to use the opportunity afforded to you and write letters to the Karmic Board.

And I can even tell you what positive help you are able to offer.

If in the name of I AM a high enough number of souls bind themselves to devote certain hours during the next six months for reciting their prayers or decrees, or saying the Rosaries and if they direct the energy of their devotional vigil on the stabilisation of the situation on earth, this will help the Karmic Board to adopt a decision enabling us to use the cosmic reserves for the stabilisation of the situation on earth.

We must be secure about the future energy payback through the energy of your prayers. So, do consider and evaluate your possibilities one more time, please.

I ask you to use this recurrent chance granted to you by Heaven.

In exchange for this you can ask in your letters about those indulgencies for you and your relatives which can be done if the Law of Karma allows this.

For example, you can use the opportunity offered in order to free from a part of karmic causes those of your relatives who suffer from chronic ailments or bad habits.

But do not forget that at first your energy will be directed on the restoration of the energy taken from the cosmic reserve for the stabilisation of the situation on earth, and only after that will the energy be directed on the realisation of your requests.

Do not undertake such obligations which you will not manage to implement. Maybe your obligations amount just to fifteen minutes of praying, but you should discharge your liabilities day after day. And this is much better than to undertake a responsibility to say prayers or the Rosaries for an hour or two and not to be able to repay your obligations even during a week.

Take a correct view of your strength and rate your strength.

The session of the Karmic Board is beginning any minute. But you can still send your letters to the Karmic Board during the fortnight to come.

I am happy that my fortunate duty is to remind you about the opportunity granted to you these days when the Karmic Board is holding a sitting on planet Earth.

The next cosmic cycle is before you, and it will last till the next session of the Karmic Board. And I hope we will succeed in keeping the balance on the planet by combined efforts.

At any rate, the Ascended Hosts are intent on exerting every effort for this. And if at least a thousandth part of this determination were inherent in just a few thousand of representatives of earthly mankind, I would be absolutely calm for the situation on planet Earth during the near months to come.

It can seem to you that every time during many hundreds of years you are frightened about the coming end of the world, but this end still does not come. And you relapse into disregarding our reminders. In reality the maintenance of the balance on planet Earth requires great efforts. And this near-destructive situation on the planet has been lasting for many hundreds and even thousands of years already.

You know that planet Earth is at the lowest point of its materiality now. For that reason, the influence of the spiritual world on the planet is greatly restricted at this lowest point. And since this lowest point of materiality takes many thousands of years, this state of being in abeyance lasts long enough. But you, those who are embodied on planet Earth, are able to exercise a lot more efforts on the physical state of the planet when it is exactly at this lowest point of materiality.

That is the reason for our tireless appeals to you.

I remind you once again that not so much effort is required in order to change the situation on the planet, because the efforts you expend have a many thousand times greater influence on the situation on earth than those of the Ascended Hosts.

Think over my words, consider your Letters of Undertaking to the Karmic Board once again and write them.

The task we are entrusting you with seems to be burdensome to you. But think over the fact that the salvation of the whole planet lies on one scale while on the other scale your transitory egoistic interests rest.

Doesn't this situation with the choice you make at times remind you of another situation with a man who goes on watching TV when his house is aflame?

We hope that within your minds the Divine rationality will predominate over your purely human affections and habits.

I AM Gautama and I have been with you this afternoon

I have brought you two pieces of news – one is sad and the other is joyful

Beloved El Morya, January 7, 2006

I AM El Morya, having come through my messenger again.

Just as the last time when we were giving the previous cycle of dictations through this messenger[8], this time I have come to announce the termination of this cycle of dictations.

This does not mean that we stop working through this or through any other messenger who has prepared his temple so as to become a pure vessel and to enable us to work through him.

Simply a certain stage has been completed, a cycle has been finished and new cycles are still in store.

I hope that the dictations received by you this time will be useful for your progress and your advancement on the Path.

One thing I have to announce today has remained incomplete and unrealised.

This concerns the new information about the dispensation on the 23rd of each month.

You remember that in my dictation from June 27, 2005 I gave you a dispensation relating to the 23rd of each month and this dispensation was in active till the end of last year.

Now the yearly cycle is over, but I have to announce to you that the dispensation will go on

---

[8] Beloved El Morya is referring to the cycle of dictations from March 4 till June 30, 2005. At that time, at the end of the cycle, in his dictation, "I congratulate you on the successful completion of this unique experiment on the transferring of the vital and timely information to the physical plane" from June 30, 2005, beloved El Morya also enunciated the completion of the cycle of dictations.

operating for a period of another year. I have succeeded in persuading the Karmic Board and in receiving its assistance in the extension of the period of this dispensation, because the energy we were receiving during the operation of the dispensation last year qualified as being satisfactory.

We are happy that you have taken advantage of the opportunity given. Many of you have. And I hope that during this year new lightbearers will join this dispensation.

Do not forget that on the 23rd of each month till the end of this year you have a chance to transmute the karma of the next month. And your efforts will be multiplied as many times as the number of lightbearers who will take part on that day in the action granted to you by Heaven.

I will not repeat to you all the conditions of this dispensation. I will only say that all the conditions stated by me in the previous message devoted to the action of this dispensation are in full force and effect.

This is a great mercy shown to you by Heaven. And I hope that this year will become a year of mighty attainments in the spiritual sphere on planet Earth.

All of us are hoping for this.

I can honestly say that we do not feel like completing this cycle of dictations.

But the Law does not allow us to spend more energy than was released.

Therefore, we hope that the next opportunity is just around the corner and will still come this year.

This is all for today. I have brought you two pieces of news – one is sad and the other is joyful. The sad one concerns the completion of the cycle of the dictations, and the joyful one refers to the extension of the operation of the dispensation on the 23rd of each month.

Everything should be balanced, and everything should be harmonised.

I am taking leave of you and I hope for future meetings.

I AM El Morya

Your consciousness is the key to your future and to the future of the whole planet

Gautama Buddha, April 18, 2006

I AM Gautama Buddha, having come to you this day.

I HAVE come to give you certain knowledge and training. As always, I am using the vessel and the opportunity afforded to me by our messenger Tatyana.

Just a short time ago we had no opportunity to give our Teaching so freely on a world-wide scale. No longer ago than two-three years no one could have supposed that the Teaching could be given in the territory of Russia. Just look how great the changes are.

We are giving our Teaching, and at the same time the situation in Russia and on the whole planet Earth is changing.

You have a chance to observe and you see how a seemingly insignificant event is capable of influencing the whole world. Probably, you do not guess, neither can you draw analogies to your lives and connect the changes taking place in them with the fact that we have now an opportunity to give our dictations. Well, we do not expect you to draw any analogies at all. Just try to observe the changes taking place in your lives and in the lives of the people around you.

Some time will pass and you will be able to discern the influence of the Ascended Hosts behind these changes. We are acting straightforwardly, and there is nothing in our actions that we do not reveal in our dictations. Without keeping anything back, we reveal in our dictations and in our Teaching the whole mechanism of our influencing both planet Earth and the changes on planet Earth.

The way things happen is very simple. You read dictations; you attend seminars which we hold with the help of our messenger and the people who expressed a wish to serve us. You receive energy and knowledge and you change your consciousness, your thinking and your vibrations.

You influence every person you meet in the street and at work. In such a manner during this year we have managed to exercise our influence on millions of people. That is why we can safely say now that the process of changing of consciousness is gaining momentum so successfully that it has been decided to hasten the process of changes on planet Earth to the maximum. This does not mean that in the near future you will be threatened by impending major disasters and natural calamities. What is more, if the process of changing of consciousness goes on at that successful rate, you will avoid many major cataclysms and disasters.

However, we cannot guarantee that no cataclysms and disasters will occur, if the opposing forces, which are ready at any sacrifice to delay the process of changes, take dynamic actions and galvanise many people into them.

Therefore, before you start any activity in your world, debate your motives in your mind carefully and try to understand the motives that predetermine the people who invite you to take part in these or those actions including the prayer practices. The energy of prayers can be craftily used for reaching goals diametrically opposite to the Divine ones.

At the present time your level of consciousness enables us to give these Teachings about the distortion of the energy of prayers. At all times there were people who directed the energy of prayers to the Supreme octaves of Light. But there were other people who used the energy of prayers while having an axe to grind. In that case they did not act in accordance with the Will of God. Moreover, the people involved in their activity created karma.

All actions in your world, all thoughts and feelings create karma. It is impossible for you not to act and, consequently, not to create karma. However, there is negative and positive karma. Negative karma extends the cycle of your lives on earth and you have to come into embodiment again and again.

Positive or good karma, in contrast, leads to the reducing of the cycle of your stay on planet Earth.

The fate of every individual and the situation on planet Earth are influenced by the balance between the positive and the negative karma which was created by humanity in the past and is being created now, at every moment of the present.

That is why we say time and again that the future of planet Earth and the process of changes on this planet depend on each of you.

No matter how grave your difficulties are, you should always remember that your existence does not terminate with the death of your physical body. Oh, you are far more than your physical bodies. Each of you has the potential to become a God. And in the course of time all of you will become Gods, except for those who voluntarily refuse to become Gods and wish to identify themselves with the physical body. You know that everything around you represents a colossal illusion. And in the grand scheme of things your task is to rise above this illusion within your consciousness. When you rise above the illusion and give up your attachments to the physical world, you continue your evolution in the Higher Worlds. If however you identify yourself with the physical world, you voluntarily doom yourself to death, because in due time the physical world will be no more and you will be unable to transit to the Higher Worlds as your consciousness does not accept them.

Thus, the key to your future and the future of the whole planet is your consciousness and the degree of your readiness to change your consciousness.

The valuable opportunity which is being given to the planet must be accepted by your consciousness. You should realise the fact of existence of the Divine opportunity and you should strive to accept this opportunity and implement it in your lives. In that case the Divine opportunity will be able to manifest itself in your physical world.

I have told you about the mechanism with the help of which we influence the physical world and change the physical world. This is the most natural way of changing which should be applied first and foremost. Any cataclysms occur because the level of human consciousness does not conform to the level which Heavens wish earthly mankind to have at a given moment. That is why we always warn you when a stepped-up work is required of you in order to change your consciousness.

At present I am happy to state that the rate of change of human consciousness satisfies the demands we raise.

Keep it up! Heavens are grateful to you. And you may fairly have high hopes for the new mercies of Heavens.

I am pleased to have met you today.

I AM Gautama Buddha. Om

The natural evolution for your souls is following the Path we are teaching mankind of earth

Lord Surya, April 24, 2006

I AM Surya, having come to you through our messenger again.

I HAVE come from the Great Central Sun to give a homily to the people of planet Earth.

For your awareness, we are giving you knowledge and information that are vital for you. We provide you with information, and every time you have a chance to receive a new pearl. After some time passes you will amusedly discover that the pearls that we have given you are enough to make a necklace. And you will be wearing this necklace till the end of your embodiment. It will impart its warmth to you and give you strength at the moments when your mind is filled with doubts about the chosen Path and the troubles of life tie you tightly up in knots of returning karma.

Don't be afraid of any difficulties you will encounter in your life. All the troubles and all the unforeseen situations are required and necessary for the development of your soul. You will be unable to evolve if you do not come across unforeseen daily situations and do not overcome the hardships of life. Only what is dead is unable to experience the delights of life and to suffer from certain manifestations of life. Thus, be thankful for everything you face in life and do not shrink from the changes.

The better your consciousness is prepared for the changes, the more easily and more quickly they occur. The reason for all your disturbances and troubles is the mistakes you made in the past. So every imbroglio you face in life must gladden you, because for you it is a chance to redeem your old errors and never to return to them.

The knowledge of the Law of Karma will enable you to alter your attitude towards any trouble. And the younger you are when you get access to the knowledge of the Law of Karma, the more easily you will accept even the most difficult situations and come out of them with honour. If you do not encounter difficulties in your life, if your life runs smoothly, then I would think over this fact if I were you. Very many people seek peace and aspire to external demonstrations of well-being. However, as soon as you get into such life conditions when everything in your life runs too smoothly, this is like a black ordeal for your soul, because you have no opportunity to evolve through external conditions and you have to descend inwardly.

Very few people know how to be all-sufficient and to contemplate only their inner being. The majority of people, after having lost their familiar surroundings full of difficulties and barriers, simply fall into depression. And this is a sign that you have entered a period of overcoming of the most severe karma – the karma between you and God.

Very many people threw out a challenge to God on an impulse of arrogance; they were so bold as to speak out against the Law of this universe. At that moment when they made bold to behave like that, nothing happened. They went on living as before and nothing changed in their lives, for a certain period of time must pass before karma starts to return. And this term is made necessary by many reasons. If you step on the Path of Initiations, the time starts running differently for you and the process of the return of karma accelerates. For ordinary people the karma of their current embodiment can be returned only in the next embodiment or even after a few embodiments. For that reason, it is very difficult to trace how the Law of Karma operates. But when you consciously enter the Path of Initiations, you receive lessons in life that allow you to trace the action of the Law of Karma during the period of literally one year. In particular instances the return of karma can speed up even more and its result can be returned in a few weeks or days.

At any rate you receive a chance to look backwards over earlier mistakes and to retrace the action of the Law of Karma. Besides, you receive training unconsciously during the day or in your sleep. You receive information from the Masters or from your Higher Self, and this information enables you to bring into confrontation the mistakes made by you in the past and the fruits - the results of these mistakes - return to you in the form of karma, or energy.

And even then, when you cannot trace sufficiently the link between your actions in the past and the consequences of these actions in the present in the form of returning karma, it is important not even to trace this link, but to accept the fact that everything happening to you takes place according to the Will of God. And the degree of your humility before the Divine Law and before the Will of God will show you the degree of your merits on the Path to God.

There are very many nuances and situations on your Path that are not susceptible of a single-value estimate by your external consciousness. Such situations sometimes contravene the code of conduct and the ethical canon existing in your society. But it is not always the case that the Divine Law coincides with the moral law of the society. So, for example, karma of a murder or any other violent act which you committed in the past must return to you. And for this purpose God can use any person whom you meet on the Path. For the purposes of the human law existing in your society, this person is a criminal and is punishable. But for the purposes of the Divine Law this human can be simply a doer of the Law of Karma. For that reason, never judge even criminals and never allow yourself to judge anybody.

At those times when a strong bond existed between your world and the Highest octaves there were people who were fundamentally incarnations of the Divine and who were capable of retracing the link between the actions of people in the past and the present. Such people acted as Divine judges and their sentencing decisions or voluntarily pardons were peremptory.

At present there are no people on earth who represent Divine incarnations in full, for any Divine incarnation in the present conditions on earth is impossible. That is why there is no chance to trace accurately the connection between your actions in the past and the problems that crop up in your life as the consequences of your past actions.

And only when you step on the Path of Initiations can you allow the Higher world to be manifested in your life. You receive knowledge about the Law of Karma and its manifestations in your lives with the help of your personal mystical bond with the Masters and your own Higher part.

That is why I have come today in order to raise again a question before your external consciousness about the necessity for you to follow the Path of Initiations. I have come from the Great Central Sun and I have brought you this message with the aim to help you understand that the natural evolution for your souls is following the Path we are teaching mankind of earth. But we cannot force anybody to follow this beaten Path.

We can only give you our knowledge and understanding, our information and energy.

Nevertheless, I am sure that a moment will come when the common sense and the internal Divine essence prevail in your life and thereupon you will gain victory after victory over the unreal part of yourselves.

I AM Surya and I wish you success on your Path!

The extension of comprehension of the Law of Karma

Beloved Kuthumi, July 6, 2006

I AM Kuthumi, having come to you today.

During that period of time while we did not meet with you I had a chance to scrutinise and to grasp the responsibility devolved upon me due to our communication. If you meditate, you will come to an inevitable conclusion that everything that happens during our communication in the process of accepting the dictations has an amazing value and requires an attentive and careful attitude. At first you may not realise this and set a low value on our messages, but as you read our messages and plunge into our energies, you will appreciate the minutes of our communication more and more and asses both the possibility of communicating with us and the quality of our messages. So, I have come today to speak with you as with old friends. And what is more, I can tell you that almost every day I meet many of you during your night's sleep in my retreat in the etheric plane. When the knowledge you receive from me in the course of our communication in the retreat finds an external confirmation in these dictations, it germinates within your consciousness, and you consciously start doing many things in the physical plane. And the eternities soak into your brain - those which could not otherwise penetrate your dense world.

And we continue our mutual work on the transformation of your physical world. This common activity does not have a connotation of an unquestioning obedience to our advice and recommendations, but implies a creative application of all the received knowledge in your life. We do not need blind followers, ready to do what they are told at our first call. We need conscientious serious-minded disciples who do not just do something thoughtlessly, but consciously analyse the received knowledge in their external consciousness and find the best case scenario for the optimal implementation of our plans.

Thus, you join in with the cosmic co-creation. And we value highly those of our disciples who do not run from one teacher to another in search of advice on how to behave in daily life situations, but are capable of raising their consciousness above day-to-day chores, of seeing the opening perspectives and setting them in motion without waiting for the ideal conditions in the physical plane to come. You are able to evolve only through the Path of overcoming both yourselves and the hardships surrounding you in your lives. You should not be afraid of life problems and lurking failures. The whole point is in your attitude to these problems and failures. The Teaching provides you with correct approaches. And you yourselves, guided by these approaches, create your lives.

You change your consciousness and alter your attitude to the problems you face in life, you analyse the barriers and problems that blow up before you and you thank God for having convinced you of your old errors and for giving you a chance to redeem them through your right attitude to the recurring problems.

You should never surrender to disappointment and depression. You receive the Teaching in order to be able to form within yourselves a right attitude to the things you come across and that accompany you in your lives. And if all of a sudden some of you with my help or, reposing on your inner intuition or a hint of your Higher Self, grasp the reason which brought into your life this or that situation relating to karma, you start thanking God times out of number for allowing you to work off your karmic debt through such an easy path.

Truly a mercy from above is unmeasured, and only you yourselves by your irrational behaviour were able to generate the reasons for the problems and disasters you face in life. At times these problems are so great, that your whole life literally passes a wet sponge even over your chance to realise your service to the Brotherhood in full. You are too burdened with the karmic loads. But the wisdom received by you through our communication helps you understand that in your future life you will be able to continue your service and will receive such circumstances in your lives that will not be too complicated and burdensome for you. This is because during your present life you have already worked off the greater part of your karmic debts. And since you have worked them off by yourselves, your children will bear a much lighter burden. It is because sometimes karmic loads that have not been worked off tend to lie as a heavy burden on children and grandchildren. Therefore, be glad over the misfortunes and calamities that rain heavily upon you. Doing so, you prepare a radiant future for yourselves in your future life and for your children and grandchildren in their present life. The right comprehension of the Law of Karma makes you happy even when, from the viewpoint of the people around you, you carry an intolerable karmic load.

The whole point is in the attitude of your external consciousness to the burden you bear. Thus, never be saddened with your problems. Let yourselves be happy with the fact that by overcoming your current difficulties you prepare a radiant future for you and your children and grandchildren.

The next generation will be much happier than you are, for many of you have taken upon yourselves karmic duties that are too big to work off during this life. You have done this purposely in order to accelerate the process of changes on planet Earth. And those people around you who point the finger of scorn at you and say that you might have sinned too much because your load is too heavy, understand nothing of the action of the Law of Karma, and their consciousness is unable to grasp the entire measure of sacrifice you have taken upon yourselves voluntarily before coming into embodiment. But we, the Ascended Hosts, value your sacrifice highly. Moreover, we are ready to respond to your requests and to help you as far as the Law allows in order to make your load less burdensome. At times, in case if good karma created by you during your current embodiment allows that, we are able to answer your call and help you in a situation when you seem to have no strength to endure it any longer. And after your call when some time has passed you look back in surprise and realise that something that was lying on your shoulders as an insurmountable burden suddenly disappeared, evaporated, fell from your shoulders. In this case never forget to glorify the Heavens and to send your gratitude. The best gratitude for us will be the service you can realise for the benefit of Life on earth.

Now I will give you a formula which will enable you to receive an indulgence for your karmic burden if your good karma allows you to do so.

So, you say:

"In the name of I AM THAT I AM, in the name of my mighty I AM Presence, in the name of my holy Christ Self (or simply in the name of Almighty God) I appeal to the Great Karmic Board with a request

to use the impetus of my good merits for the purpose of wiping out the karmic debt which has led to... (further you should describe the situation for which you wish to receive help from the Karmic Board).

May all the things take place in accordance with the Will of God."

You can write a letter, read your call out loud and burn the letter, addressing it to the Karmic Board. If the amount of your accumulated good karma allows it and the Karmic Board thinks your request is fit to comply with, your karmic situation will be resolved to a greater or lesser degree.

In accordance with the opportunity given to you earlier, you will be called in your higher body during your night's sleep to the meeting of the Karmic Board and your soul will have to confirm your request which you wrote in your external consciousness. Sometimes there are cases when the external consciousness of a human cannot endure the karmic load any longer, but the soul of this human refuses help. In this case the Karmic Board heeds the opinion of your soul. Thus, if your request is not entertained, you can talk to your soul after some time and try to come to an agreement with it on this question. I highly recommend you to practise conversations with your soul and to write letters to the Karmic Board only after you and your soul have reached an agreement between yourselves.

You are multilayered beings. You have many bodies. Therefore, you need to reach harmony and unity between all your bodies. The bodies of the majority of humans are unbalanced to such an extent that you cannot even realise how you should act in the best interests of all the bodies. Stop associating yourselves just with what you see in the mirror. You are much more than your physical body. And the next stage in the evolution of humanity will be the comprehension of your higher nature and the creation of harmonious conditions for your higher nature to manifest itself, because the conditions you are living in now at times absolutely do not promote harmony to settle within your higher bodies. This is the next stage of development of mankind. But already now you should worry about creating the environment suitable for the harmonious development of all your bodies.

I have given you much new information today. And I am leaving you with a hope for new meetings.

I AM Kuthumi

A teaching on the karmic responsibility for your actions in the sphere of translating the texts of the dictations and in the sphere of managing cash funds

Sanat Kumara, July 9, 2006

I AM Sanat Kumara, having come to you again.

From this day forth till the end of the current cycle of dictations I want you every day before reading a dictation to invocate the electronic presence of the Master giving this dictation. This seemingly simple technique will enable you to feel our presence and will present quite a new view of many theses of our messages, because the presence of the Masters during the reading of the messages will many times magnify the effect you experience while reading them. This is a special dispensation, and it will be active still for some time after the completion of this cycle of dictations. You will be able to judge by your gut sense whether this dispensation is still operating or not.

So, in order to invocate the presence of the Master giving a message you should pronounce either aloud or to yourself:

"**In the name of I AM THAT I AM I invocate the electronic presence of…** (insert the name of the Master giving the message)"

Try to use this dispensation beginning from today's dictation. Read this dictation to the end and then reread it after having made a call and you will feel the difference.

I recommend that you always make such calls before reading the messages we give through this messenger. The operation of the call will be manifested when possible and necessary.

All the Masters can manifest their electronic presence, and the degree of this presence will be in direct ratio to your ability to perceive our vibrations and to the readiness of your higher bodies to distinguish our vibrations.

You know that sometimes we give our messages at a higher level and sometimes we give them at a slightly lower level. And this is not always predicated upon the quality of conductibility of the bodies of our messenger. It is just because there are different levels of development of consciousness of individuals embodied now. And different individuals are capable of perceiving different information and different energetic components of the messages.

We thoroughly verify the information given. And when your external consciousness starts analysing the information, this does not always happen to be useful. It is because any critical perception of information cuts short the flux of energy. And the reading of our messages becomes useless for you. A message as such energises within you a directivity to the energies of the Masters, and you distinguish our energies at the moment of reading the messages. There are keys that energise your higher conductors, and you become able to perceive not only the informational component of the messages but their energetic component as well. This explains the fact that our messages are impossible to retell. A retelling does not carry in itself the keys hidden within the body of the message. You take in our messages as a text written with the help of symbols of this or that language. However, it is not exactly so. A message carries in itself hidden keys. And when you translate our messages into different languages these keys can be lost. Everything depends on the internality of the translator. And if the translator is attuned to us, the translation in itself carries our vibrations. If not, the translation carries only the informational component. This explains the fact that even though you speak another language, you still receive the energetic component of the messages when listening to the dictations being read by our messenger and not understanding the words. You feel the energies and vibrations of the Masters.

If you read our messages translated into your native language you can lose this energetic component. Accordingly, I recommend those who translate our dictations into other languages in the future, before starting the translation, to invocate the electronic presence of the Master, the translation of whose dictation you are going to realise. I also advise you to start the translation in a balanced state after a good meditation or a prayer practice.

Any imperfections you have are imposed on the text of the translation. And if you happen to distort the text of the dictation at the process of the translation, the karmic responsibility for the distortion of the Words of the Masters falls on you.

Yet, this karmic responsibility of yours can be neutralised by good karma which you acquire at the moment of translating the dictations into other languages and distributing them.

But you should bear in mind that good karma is acquired by you only if your motive is pure and you really do translations in order to spread our Teaching, but not in order to earn money.

The question of interrelation with money is one of considerable nicety and difficulty. In reality money comes to you not when you perform some work for the Brotherhood.

But when doing some work for the Brotherhood you receive opportunities, enabling the energy of money to pay back the energetic consumption you incurred while being involved in the work for the Brotherhood.

Everything in this world is based on energy exchange. And any stagnation of energy leads to the shortage of monetary energy. When you have money you should think where you should spend it. Any accumulation of monetary energy is not useful and represents a sign of karma of incorrect attitude to money. Think about how you should dispose of the money you have. And if you spend this money on pleasure, next time you will not receive the payback of the monetary energy.

In contrast, if you spend your store of money on good causes, the flux of monetary energy will be intensified, notwithstanding the fact of how much effort you apply to earn the money. You will get a windfall or somebody will give you money under any pretense.

Do manage monetary energy correctly. The more you give disinterestedly, the more you receive.

But you should always remember that you are responsible for how much and to whom you give your money, because in the case that the money you give is used not on good deeds, the karma of the misuse of monetary energy will devolve upon you.

And in contrast, if you contribute money on good deeds, good karma of correct use of your money will give you a chance to dispose of this good karma at your sole discretion.

Therein lies the principal of the church tithe. It is, essentially, a very right and exact principle, but only if the church or any other religious organisation spends your tithe on good deeds, not on multiplying their own property.

The principle of the reasonable and right use of the Divine energy is manifested in everything, and monetary energy is in no way different from any other kind of energy.

One kind of energy turns smoothly into another kind of energy. And your tithe, if you manage it correctly, provides you with the manifestation of opportunities in the physical plane. These opportunities can pour upon you in the form of a flood of cash, a joyful future for your children, your own health and the health of your nearest and dearest.

Good karma can be used also for the purpose you personally want it to. For this you are given a chance to write letters to the Karmic Board.

Today I have given you a Teaching on the karmic responsibility for your actions in the sphere of translating the texts of the dictations and in the sphere of managing cash funds.

And this vital Teaching requires an immediate use in your lives.

And now let me leave you and good-bye for the moment.

I AM Sanat Kumara. Om

A teaching on prophets and prophecies

John the Beloved, July 13, 2006

I AM John the Beloved. I am known to you as the author of the Apocalypse. And I have come again in order to give a Teaching posited on the internal knowledge – the knowledge that was easy of access only to prophets and mystics. Such people still exist in this day and age, but they are often mistaken for charlatans of all persuasions who declare themselves prophets or clairvoyants, or psychics, while the threshold of their perception of the Divine World is so low that at times it would be better for their future if they stopped their prophecies and fell silent.

What do you think – is there any karma carried by prophets and what that karma is? I will tell you, since I know very well what kind of karma we are talking about.

There is no difference between prophesying and any other activity in which you can be engaged in the physical world. And prophets come in all shapes and sizes. There are prophets making prophecies from the Light, and there are prophets who soothsay from darkness. Each prophet chooses for himself which forces to serve.

Soothsaying is a gift of contact with the invisible world. This gift is acquired during not just one embodiment. And when this gift is granted to a person prophesying from God, this person usually realises the full karmic responsibility laid on his shoulders. Prophesies represent probabilities of occurrence of events sensed from the higher plane. Depending on the plane and the level at which the prophecy is sensed, it can be more or less accurate. But as long as familiar things of the physical plane are missing in the higher plane, the gift of prophecy presupposes a gift of events' representation based on the impressions from the contact with the higher plane.

Since the human mind is involved in the process of the representation of impressions, a distortion of information takes place at this stage and the authenticity of the prophecy is lost. In view of the fact that I wrote the Apocalypse with symbols, I managed to avoid the karma laid on the prophet in the case that the oracle failed. And each expert in forecasting provides his veiled knowledge in the form of verses, parables and quatrains. This is very fair, as it makes it possible to avoid karma if the prophecy is erroneous.

There are other prophets who use human interest in oracles and soothsay in down-to-earth language, positing their prophecies on the knowledge they draw from the low levels of the astral plane or while being under the effect of mind-altering drugs.

These prophecies do not contain big truths. And they do not come true, as a rule. The probability of such prophecies coming true is fifty per cent. This is just the case when people say, "There's many a slip between the cup and the lip".

However, the aspiration to satisfy human interest in soothsaying puts a great karmic responsibility upon such prophets and clairvoyants. In the case that the prophecy is incorrect, the more people know about this prophecy, the greater the responsibility is. The point is in the fact that any prophecy programmes the consciousness of people who give credit to it. And if there are heaps of people who wish to believe the prophecy, these people create by their consciousness an opportunity for the realisation of such a prophecy. And if a phenomenon predicted by a forecaster does not coincide with the Divine vision, but is realised and takes place due to the momentum of human consciousness involved in this phenomenon, karma lies both upon the forecaster and those people who contribute to the realisation of this phenomenon by their consciousness.

That is why any oracle is a two-edged sword. If a prophecy alters the Divine plane for the better, the realisation of such a prophecy brings good karma to all the people who take part in its realisation by their consciousness. If the Divine plane is worsened as a result of the prophecy, a negative karma of the prophecy is created.

Soothsaying is a phenomenon as dual as everything in your world.

And those people who come under the influence of the energy of the prophecies of false foretellers create negative karma.

The prophets of Light have always been out of favour, because the majority of people did not like the oracles coming through them. People have always treated such prophets cautiously. They would rather have no dealings with them and try to quash them physically. The karma of despatching a prophet of Light fell as a heavy burden on the next generations.

In contrast, any veneration of God's prophets brought good karma to the family of the person who showed hospitality to a prophet.

True prophets were always messengers of God, and their mission was necessary in order to contribute to the right development of human consciousness. Those who declared themselves as prophets without having been stamped with the seal of God incurred a descending heavy karma on them. Therefore, always observe and examine and do not let yourselves get involved in any activity relating to prophecies if it is not from God, if it is demonic.

I am giving you this Teaching, since, although hundreds of years have passed from the moment of my incarnation, it has not lost its reality. In contrast, it has acquired actuality, as many visionaries and clairvoyants have appeared who do far more harm than good. And if you are involved in their activity, resort to their services and pay for them, you create karma of a wrong action.

I have come to give you this important Teaching on the true and false prophets in order to help you to be able in your consciousness to approach everything you meet on your Path in this sphere with your eyes open.

It is very important where you direct your energy. None of the false prophets would be able to foretell if you did not give them the energy of your attention and your money, thus encouraging them to take up this ungodly business. False prophets are the children of impure human consciousness, ignorance and superstition.

And now that the body of the Teaching has been given, I would like to make a prophecy relating to your future. Before my coming to you, I and the other Ascended Masters were pondering whether it was worth giving you this prophecy through this messenger, as we had to consider the purity of the conductors and the degree of distortion of the information which might happen. We have decided to run a risk, and so I am starting.

In this anxious time in which you are living, you constantly think about many things and especially about the future of your planet, whether there is a threat of the next global cataclysm on it. That is why it is very important for you to hear that it is unlikely that any global cataclysm will take place during the life of the generation living now. But everything can change, if you do not endeavour to transform your consciousness daily. The stable equilibrium on the planet which has been achieved so far depends for its existence on the fact that many people have raised in their consciousness to such a level where they are able to think positively and to direct their efforts to the public weal, to the Good and the Light. And if the number of such people increases with each year, no global cataclysm will occur during the life of the next generation either, because each preceding generation paves the way for the next one. And by your consciousness you are preparing a steady development for all the living on earth during the next cosmic cycle.

I wish you to successfully continue keeping your consciousness on this high level.

I AM John the Beloved, with great respect to your I AM lifestreams

The time is ripe not to speak about God, but to act in your lives in obedience to the Divine Law

Lord Lanello, December 24, 2006

I AM Lanello, having come today to give you one more message. The advantage of our messages is in their opportunity to influence a mainstream audience. We give moderate information comprehensible for millions of people. And in the near future we sincerely expect millions of people to trust in us, the Ascended Masters, and to start to transform the illusion of the physical plane under our guidance. The time has finally come for the transformation of the physical world to take place in accordance with the Divine plan for the current time. The age which is triumphing now requires transformations in all the spheres of human life. The above is true not only of the spiritual sphere, but also of politics, the economy, education and public health. Everything must be transformed under the influence of new energies and new vibrations that are descending into the physical plane now.

And if before certain transformations required a centuries-old period in order to take place, at present the realisation of the necessary changes will be just a matter of years. Such are both the dictate of the present time and the decision of the Supreme Cosmic Council for planet Earth. So, strive to change yourselves and to give up as soon as possible the traits and imperfections preventing you from advancing on the Path of transformations. Only when you purify yourselves from bygone energies and get rid of karmic accumulations, will you be able to discern the tasks ahead of you and the things you are required to realise. But unless and until you refuse to accept this within yourselves and continue to dig in your toes, tightly holding on to your outdated stereotypes of thinking and old imperfections, you will not be able to take a move to the beautiful horizons of the New Day destined for you.

Do dare to meet eye-to-eye with yourself and with your imperfections. If my words wind you up and it seems to you that you are the very perfection incarnate and that nobody, including the Ascended Masters, has a right to lecture you, then you are lacking the essential quality on your Path – Divine humility and obedience. It seems to you that it is you who are the architects of your fortune and can do with yourself whatever you like. Yet, you must realise the Divine logic. Your God the Father is a very caring and loving parent. In this respect you are very lucky with your Father in Heaven. And insofar as He loves you greatly, he cannot allow you to go on doing your soul harm at that rate. Trust your Father and humbly submit to His Will.

The change of cosmic cycles is a compulsory requirement of time. Thus, the things which obstruct the Great Transition within you must be overcome by yourselves. Don't oppose, as only when you within yourselves make up your mind to get rid of everything unwanted, moth-eaten and negative and ask God to free you from your karmic load, only then are the Ascended Hosts able to rush to rescue you and to help you in overcoming a centuries-old accretion of negative energy.

But if you recalcitrate and defend your imperfections and bad habits, nobody will be able to help you – neither God nor man.

Penitence and confession have always been the tools which allow a soul to be purged and follow the Divine Path.

It is not always that people who speak much about God follow the Divine Path. Those who spend most part of the day in prayers do not always follow the Divine Path.

The time has come when you, each of you, must follow in your life the commandments given by the prophets, those tables of the law that were written on the stone tablets in the days of Moses.[9]

Analyse this Decalogue and search your behaviour. Do many of you truly obey these laws in your lives? Do many of you act in life in obedience to the Divine Law?

The time is ripe not to speak about God, but to act in your lives in obedience to the Divine Law.

And for many of you this will be much more difficult than to attend church services, pray and keep a fast. However such is the dictate of time. Stop playing cat-and-mouse at least with yourselves. Be on your best behaviour when you are alone with yourself, just as you would behave with other people, and behave toward other people just as you would behave if you had God the Father in front of you.

Every minute and every second of your life all your actions and all your thoughts are being unceasingly written into the Akashic Records. And when you manage to see these Chronicles, you will discover rapidly why the things happening in your life take place

---

[9] 1. You shall have no other gods before Me. 2. You shall not make for yourself a carved image - any likeness of anything that is in heaven above, or that is in the earth beneath, or that is in the water under the earth. 3. You shall not take the name of the LORD your God in vain. 4. Remember the Sabbath day, to keep it holy. 5. Honour your father and your mother. 6. You shall not murder. 7. You shall not commit adultery. 8. You shall not steal. 9. You shall not bear false witness against your neighbour. 10. You shall not covet your neighbour's house; you shall not covet your neighbour's wife, nor his male servant, nor his female servant, nor his ox, nor his donkey, nor anything that is your neighbour's. (Deut. 5:6-21)

this way and not another way and why you are pursued by your ill luck and disasters.

All the disasters and everything which surrounds you in life were created by you in the past. The Law of Karma operates faultlessly.

That is why the understanding of the fact that you face in life the consequences of your own past actions and that nobody except you is blameworthy for the things happening to you will be the utmost achievement in your lives. And none of the events of your life is comparable in order of importance to this discovery which you will make in your heart.

And when you see the operation of the Great Law, you will understand that God is very gracious to you and the actions you committed in the past must be punished with much more destitution, and many more diseases and misfortunes. And you will be stunned with the mercy of the Father and will experience full humility and obedience before His Will and His Law.

And only when you repent inside your heart will you be able to know the Kingdom of Heaven and follow the Path without taking the wrong turning and shirking the responsibilities you took upon yourselves before coming into embodiment.

And now I am ready to remind you that Christmas Eve is coming.[10] The western part of humanity celebrates this Christmas holiday as one of the most significant in the year. That is why on the eve of this holiday you should think about the fact that inside each of you Christ can be born as soon as you give your Higher Self a chance to act through you.

Your Higher Self cannot start acting through you as long as you oppose and disobey the Divine Law of this

[10] In western Christianity Christmas is celebrated on the 25th of December. In Orthodoxy Christmas is celebrated on the 7th of January.

universe. But from the moment when you in your heart decide to obey the Law, your Higher Self becomes able to act through you and your actions become actions of a Christ-being in manifestation.

I wish you a happy Christmas and I wish that each of you finds a Christ within you!

I AM Lanello with Love to you

One more vital point is added to the dispensation on the 23rd of each month

Gautama Buddha, December 25, 2006

I am Gautama Buddha, having come to you again to give a new message inspired by the force of Love that I, as well as the other Ascended Masters, feel towards you, people of Earth embodied at present. The time is very stressful and the turn of the year is a time of special importance and complexity. It is at the turn of the solar cycle that we come and give you our training, since everything we plant on the growing sun will germinate in spring and summer when the next solar cycles come which are the day of the vernal equinox and the day of summer solstice. The old is nearing its completion and the new is beginning to show, and this new is absolutely gorgeous!

I can say this as I am directly relevant to the future that is to come very soon. We are happy that there is a sufficient number of human individuals who wish to serve us, the Ascended Masters, and we are able to materialise our plans together with you.

I am standing in front of you in a great state because today at the Session of the Karmic Board a vital event has occurred, and this event will not be long in influencing the life of each tellurian. It has been decided during the session that each tellurian who has achieved a certain level of consciousness will be able to spend a part of the energy he frees during praying or while serving Life in order to enable the rest of humanity of earth to achieve the level of consciousness that is necessary at the current stage of the evolutionary development as soon as possible. We time this important decision to coincide with the dispensation of the 23rd of each month and now, starting from the 23rd of January of next year, one more fundamental point is being added in counterpart to the guidelines of this important dispensation that are still in operation during the entire period of next year. Each of you, who wish, can direct your energy onto the transmutation of karma of those who have decelerated their development and are unable to understand many Divine Truths. This can relate to your loved ones, your relatives and even strangers to whom you feel a special affinity. On the 23rd of each month of next year you can make a call and transmute that karma that prevents the person chosen by you from the achieving the next level of consciousness. For the time being each of you can practise this dispensation for one person only, for example, this can be your spouse, your child or any of your parents or any person whom you want to help.

We hope sincerely that this new Divine opportunity will let both us and you accelerate the pace of raising the level of consciousness of earthly mankind. Just picture that by the end of next year, after the completion of the annual cycle and the session of the Karmic Board, the number of people who will have reached the level of consciousness that allows them to serve us consciously will double! In such a way by the end of the year we will have a chance to double the number of our devotees – the people capable of taking upon themselves a responsibility for both the planet and the evolutionary development of all the living creatures on earth.

I am happy to have got this joyful decision over to you! And now I am ready to give you a small piece of information that will allow you to orient yourselves in the current state of things in the world. What is meant here is the catastrophic increase of the level of negative vibrations at the end of the year. A lot of people are seized with heaviness, and very many celebrate their Christmas and New Year holidays at a very low vibration level, drinking alcohol and being engaged in indecent and reproachful actions. All these things create an extra portion of the planetary karma, which can bring irreparable disasters on some continents. That is why I turn to you as always at the end of the year with a request to keep balance first of all within yourselves and to devote as much effort as possible to the balancing of the planetary karma and the karma of your country. If you feel such an internal need, you can devote every day remaining till the end of the current year to your prayer practice with a vengeance. Do not hesitate even to obtain leave in order to work for the good of planet Earth at home in privacy or with a group of like-minded people. Read Rosaries, read other prayers or practise meditation. Send out your Love and Gratitude to Earth. Picture Mother-Earth as an alive being allowing you to live and to evolve and taking care of you. Send out your Love to Earth and to those elementals which maintain the human evolution on Earth.

At the end of every year we ask you for extra energy you are able to give us, and this in its turn enables us to balance the situation on the planet and to avoid many cataclysms.

That is why I come and turn to you with a request as an entity that wields power and keeps the balance on planet Earth.

I AM Buddha, and I am glad that many of you have decided and darted to the path of serving humanity of earth, having forgotten about your own problems and your own difficulties and misfortunes.

In reality, only when you are immersed in serving Life, all your petty concerns leave you one after another and one fine day you realise that you are free from all these trifling and unnecessary things that burdened you before. But that was another life, a life of a person egoistic and absorbed in his own problems. But now you represent a being of Light anxious about happiness and harmony on the planet.

May the world be well!

May all the living creatures inhabiting our dearly loved planet Earth be happy. Om.

I AM Gautama Buddha

You must constantly analyse the consequences of your actions and stop trying to teach in those places where your teaching will be immediately dragged through the mire

Beloved Kuthumi, December 26, 2006

I AM Kuthumi, having come to you today through our messenger. I have to give you yet another piece of our Teaching that you have to assimilate because the time for it has come. The present time is such that every manifestation of the Divinity you meet in life becomes a feast-day for your souls, because your souls have been aching for the Divine world whence they came and where it is time to return now. That is why I am always happy to forward a message from the Divine world to you and to give you short precepts.

I know that many of you love me and speak with me. And when you are attuned to my wavelength I almost never fail to hear you and to perceive your thoughts because this is the way I serve. Hence, I know about many of you. And I am aware of the problems you are overburdened with. That is why I would like to do my level best and to do everything in my power in order to show you the roots of the problems cropping up before you and to provide you with a spark necessary for you to be able to overcome within you the reasons for your difficulties.

That is why today we will talk about what is vital and topical for many of you. And this is connected with your interrelations with those people around you who do not understand and accept your teaching, your edifications, your pattern of life and your system of world-view. Unfortunately, all humans are at absolutely different stages of progress. And by the level of your consciousness many of you still belong to the previous fourth root race. The majority of you belong to different sub-races of the fifth root race, and there is a certain number, a very small number of individuals who belong to the final sub-races of the fifth root race and even a smaller number of individuals belonging to the sixth root race, whose time has not come yet, but whose first pathfinders, especially impatient ones, undertake their pioneer embodiments at present.

The history of the development of the races is a matter for a time-consuming discussion and will not be a subject of this dictation. All I want is to direct your attention to an indisputable fact that all of you are standing at different stages of your evolutionary development. And that is why the difference in your consciousness is sometimes so great and the spheres of your interests and the level of your consciousness differ to such an extent that it seems at times that you speak different languages. For that reason, when you yet again have a desire to start giving a teaching or to propagandise your views among those who, as you think, need to be preached, remember this dictation and call to mind the words of Jesus "Do not cast your pearls before swine".[11]

All that is given must be given according to the level of consciousness. And many things that seem to be so obvious to you that you have already stopped to pay attention to them can appal the people who are remote from your views. What is worse, this can create in them a whole gamut of negative emotions and even actions. And who do you think will bear the karma of these negative manifestations? If you have not guessed

---

[11] Give not that which is holy unto the dogs, neither cast your pearls before the swine, lest haply they trample them under their feet, and turn and rend you. Mat 7:6

yet, I will prompt you: the karma will lie on you. It is because a human standing at a higher stage of evolutionary development takes full karmic responsibility not only for his/her own actions, but also for the actions of the people whom he/she provokes to wrong actions.

This does not mean that people whom you provoke are freed from their karma for the wrong actions at all. I only want to say that the greater part of karma will lie on you because it is you who provoke them to perform these wrong actions. Therefore, before you start preaching and giving anybody a piece of advice about how to act in life think a good many times whether it is worth doing.

Your responsibility is directly proportional to the stage of the evolutionary ladder you occupy. This does not mean that you should shrink into yourself and stop communicating with people and speaking on spiritual topics with them. Simply, you must constantly analyse the consequences of your actions and stop trying to teach in those places where your teaching will be immediately dragged through the mire.

Think about my words. And always remember that your own behaviour in life, the way you react to these or those life situations and disturbances, serve as the best model. All your preaching will lie in your actions. And by the fruits of your actions people will recognise in you that person whom it is worth heeding and whose advice it is worth seeking. So, I am again driving at the fact that the only person in this world with whom it behoves you to occupy yourself seriously is yourself. And you yourselves are the most worthy recipient of all your forces and abilities.

Do not think that somebody acts imperfectly and do not think of how he should act. Concentrate on yourself and think why actions and words of other people irritate you. Isn't it because everything that irritates you is in evidence within you as a manifestation of your past wrong actions?

The physical world around you is a mirror reflecting your imperfect consciousness. Thus, it would be natural to assume that if someone regularly meets with ignorance and misunderstanding, these qualities are present in him/her. And if you are all the time subject to the spiteful attacks of other people, it means that the negative energy making people act so towards you is present within you.

We have covered today's material many times. And you have certainly heard and read about this many times. However, your thoughts, your own thoughts that you send me, make me repeat again this small Teaching to you and remind you about those Truths that you know well but for some reason do not risk to apply to yourselves.

I am happy with the opportunity given to repeat this Teaching to you. And I will be even happier if some of you are able to put this Teaching into practice. And even if it seems to you that everything I have told about has nothing to do with you, still do not hurry to put this dictation away and to shelve it. Try to reread this message at least thrice on different days, at different times of the day and in different states of your consciousness. And I think that while reading it for the third time you will start to understand that this dictation is directly relevant to you.

Trust me, I know human psychology very well, and at times it is a great pleasure to me to think out the puzzles composed from those psychological problems that you yourselves have created during thousands and thousands of embodiments on earth. However, I am always glad to help you. And I always answer your requests which you sincerely pronounce in your heart when looking at my picture or which you risk to write on paper and send me by the irreproachable post where our angels work. Do you happen to know that when you burn the letter and make a call to the angels of protection to deliver the letter to me or to any other Ascended Master the physical letter burns, but its energetic higher substance is momentarily delivered at the address specified by you?

I have been happy to give you a small Teaching today.

I AM Kuthumi, with great Love towards you and with a desire to help

A message at the beginning of the year

Gautama Buddha, January 1, 2007

I AM Gautama Buddha, having come to you again today, at the beginning of a new yearly cycle.

Every time a new annual cycle begins we come to give you instructions related to the new cycle of time. And I have come today to give such an instruction.

You know that a yearly cycle is subject to the operation of the Law of Karma in such a way that karma descends not in one lump but is spun out throughout the whole yearly period. Every month you receive the return of a certain amount of karma. This way you have an opportunity to work off your past karma gradually, year after year and month after month. If you had a chance to immediately work off the entire amount of your karma - your negative energy, the energy you distorted in your previous lives - you would not be able to endure it. Your bodies would be torn to shreds momentarily. That is why the action of the Law is such that every moment of your life you are given a chance to come to grips with the exact amount of negative energy of your past with which you can cope at that moment. You are never given more than you can endure. Therefore, you are simply required to be reconciled to the Law of this universe and to wait humbly for the return of the karmic energy that you created yourselves and that is given to you in cycles in order to be worked off.

A new year is considered by convention to be the beginning of the working off of a new layer of the energies of the past. By completing a year after a year successfully you work off your past karma and charge toward a new level of consciousness. And if it were not for the new karma that you are tirelessly creating, just a few years would be enough for you to get free from the lion's share of your past karma.

But not all of you can sensibly dispose of your Divine energy and the time of your embodiment. That is why for many of you the amount of negative energy that you work off through suffering, diseases and misfortunes is immediately replenished with new karma that you are untiringly creating by wrong actions and wrong choices in your lives.

And if it were not for the Divine mercy, you would be completely deprived of an opportunity to progress onward – such huge karma many of you are creating in your lives. However, owing to the Divine mercy, this karma does not return to you at once, but is waiting for a favourable opportunity when you are able to meet with the negative energy of the past and not only to withstand your karmic burden but also to think over the reason why so many misfortunes rain thick upon you all at once. In such a way many of you will be able to comprehend the existence of the Supreme Law and will wish to aspire with all your being to obey this Law.

Many of you have reached such a level of consciousness that they appeal to the Karmic Board with requests to speed up the return of karma so as to have a chance to work off the maximum amount of karma during the current embodiment and to acquire an opportunity to serve at a new level of consciousness free from karma.

The only thing I would like to warn you about is the following: after you have written such letters and the return of your karma accelerates, do not forget what you yourselves have asked about and do not repine at your unhappy lot. The fact is that the process of karma descending, when being sped up by your request, can be suspended exactly the same way and returned to its natural flow. Do not forget about your requests, and if you have been too hasty and overrated your strength, write another letter to the Karmic Board and ask it not to speed up the process of the descending of your karma in the future.

Very many of you do not realise the obligations which you undertook upon yourselves while being in your higher body, at the level of your soul. Thus, when you face difficulties in your life and these difficulties exhaust you too much, do debate this matter in your mind. Talk to your Higher Self, seek its advice. In any case, owing to the great mercy of Heaven, the process of karma descending can be regulated by you. It is especially important if you have good karma created by helping living creatures and the Masters, because your good karma can be always used in order to mitigate the heaviness of your karmic burden.

As soon as you have realised the action of the Law of Karma and you aspire to act in your life in harmony with this Law, you meet one of the predominant constituents of your further progress, and the mercy of Heaven will not fail to come to your help at your first call.

Pitiful are those individuals who disregard the Law of Karma and go on living by the principle:" After me the deluge".

You should think about this expression of yours. It might be that in your next embodiment you will get into the deluge that you drew upon yourselves.

Think about how many misfortunes and problems people could avoid if every minute of their life they thought not only about the consequences of their actions but also about the consequences of their thoughts and feelings.

One of the objects of our messages is exactly to teach you to be aware of your every action, every thought and feeling, as there are no secrets for God and for the cosmic Law and all your thoughts as well as your actions and deeds are recorded in the Akashic Records. You can play cat-and-mouse with one another and hide your true motives and your negative thoughts. God sees everything and it is impossible for you to hide even the slightest secret workings of your heart from Him.

And it would not be amiss for you to make it a rule to constantly feel the presence of an invisible witness near you who keeps watch over your actions and even over the workings of your heart. Then you will be able to approach all your actions and choices in life in a more responsible manner.

And I wish to give you one more important piece of advice. If you are guided by it, you will be able to increase the percentage of worked off karma very quickly. Every time you face a choice as how to act in your life, try to understand the motive you are driven by while making this choice. And if you strive to do something for your personal benefit, it is a wrong motive and the result of your choice will increase your karmic burden.

If you are guided in your choices by the motive to do good for other people and other living creatures, then even if it seems to you that your choice can cause damage to you and is unprofitable according to all the human laws and from the viewpoint of elementary human logic – never say die. From the viewpoint of the Divine logic you will make a correct choice, and this choice will inevitably lead to the easing of your karmic burden. You lose in the small things, but you win in the great.

For example, you are driving along a mountainous road and a person who needs your help appears on the road in front of you. You expend time in helping him and lose this time. The sun sets and you are delayed on the way. But if you do not yield to the feeling of annoyance, tomorrow a new gateway will open for you of which you were not aware before, and this gateway will speed up your movement a lot and you will get to the right place much earlier than you planned.

This is how the Law of Karma operates.

Never think about the profit you will get if you perform good actions. May your karmic debts and merits be counted by those heavenly beings that must act by virtue of their position. Simply perform good actions and do not think about a reward.

I am glad to have reminded you at the beginning of the year about the Great Law existing in this universe and I hope that I have done it, as always, just in time.

I AM Gautama Buddha

A talk about the healing of the soul and the body

Beloved Hilarion, January 4, 2007

I AM Lord Hilarion, having come to you today.

As always, I have come to give you instructions necessary for the internal work each of you performs when communing with yourself in the inmost recesses of your heart. How rare are such minutes when you are on your own. All your concerns pale into insignificance and you suddenly find yourself alone with your thoughts.

Think of how good it would be if you communed with yourself not just from time to time, but had a chance to communicate with yourself every day, devoting just a few minutes to this communication with your heart.

I, Lord Hilarion, remember the minutes when, being in incarnation and leading a solitary life in the backwoods, I had a chance to observe myself as if from outside all day long. I understood that I was flesh and blood in incarnation with all the functions of my body. But at the same time I began to realise that within me there was another man who was not connected directly with the functions of my physical body. It was a strange feeling of double personality. I was on earth in incarnation and at the same time I understood that I was immortal. I was eternal. I was thrown upon my own resources in that incarnation and I tried to understand the reason for my being, but at the same time I was much more than my physical body. At bottom, my physical body was just like body armour enabling my Higher Self to dwell within me.

And during those minutes of clear understanding of who I was in reality my consciousness raised to inconceivable heights from where I saw clearly the unity of the entire biosphere existing on earth. I clearly saw the unity of all the kingdoms of nature, angels and elementals. During those joyful minutes of tranquil commune with my heart I felt around me thousands of beings, invisible to the human eye but nevertheless living, who were speaking to me and trying to get in touch with me. At those minutes I experienced unity with every bug, with all the birds and animals.

How beautiful it was! And this was possible only when I was alone with myself. There was nobody around me except animals, birds, angels and elementals.

Then people came to me. Those people were seeking healing from me. They aspired to come to me in order to get hold of a grain of my quiet happiness and serenity. But as soon as those people with their concerns and problems arrived in my world, the dwellers of my world hid, because the vibrations of those people were unfamiliar and hostile to the vibrations of these dwellers, as well as to my vibrations to which they had become accustomed during the period of our quiet communication.

I rendered help to many people. I healed their souls. I prepared remedies from herbs and I gave them those arcana. But it was not herbs that healed their damaged and feeble bodies. It was the people who cured themselves once their consciousness rose to the level where they began to realise what harm they had done to their souls and physical bodies by committing wrong actions and tolerating wrong feelings.

When non-divine feelings take possession of a person it is much like a whirlwind devastating his higher bodies. And if hatred, sorrow, sadness, envy, jealousy and other negative feelings do often possess you, every time hurricane after hurricane dashes through your higher bodies and finally your higher bodies come to a very ragged condition and can no longer serve you as conductors of the Divine energy. And you start suffering from those diseases that force you to seek healing from many herbalists and healers. And you will be incredibly lucky if you happen to meet on your path a healer who will cure not your body but your soul.

This is because first of all it is your higher bodies that need healing - your emotional body, your memory or etheric body and your mental body. It is these bodies that represent a more mutable part of you and that are destroyed first of all, being constantly affected by negative thoughts and feelings.

The destruction and the diseases of the physical body are just the results of the damage and diseases of the higher bodies. That is why it is your soul that needs to be healed first. It is necessary to bring you to the understanding that you yourselves with your wrong actions, thoughts and feelings throw your physical body into a disease.

Many of you go on keeping aggression in your heart, blaming doctors, relatives, your jobs and your bosses for your poor state of health. But this is a wrong concept. The first step towards your healing should be your understanding that no one is guilty for your diseases but you. And you yourselves provoked all your diseases when you raged, did harm to other people, used foul language, performed evil deeds, ate and drank products polluting your organism.

You yourselves are the reason for your illnesses. And when you come to the understanding of this simple truth, you make the first and the main move towards your healing.

The next step is to make a decision never to perform such actions that led you to the disease. For some people this means getting rid of negative thoughts, for others, negative feelings and for some, negative deeds.

You should desire to get rid of everything that was the reason for the ailment of your soul and body. And only after that are you ready for the next step – the step when you sincerely call to God in your broken heart and ask for the healing of your soul and physical body from ailments.

Very many of you are in such a sorry plight that it already does not seem possible to cure the physical body in the current life. However, when you understand the causes of your illness and set the correct pattern of behaviour and mindset, this will bring peace to your soul. And in your next life you will be able to realise the reason for your diseases much faster, and from your youth you will take care not only of your physical body, but also of the right pulsebeat of your thoughts and feelings.

It is a rare case when a person starts to understand by himself the direct interconnection between his ailments and the deeds he performed in youth and in his mature years. And if we could show many of you the obscene deeds you committed, many would be surprised because it is impossible to tolerate things like that in your enlightened time.

Yet, sorry to say, your civilisation is oriented to ruin your soul. And many of the so-called feature movies affect your higher bodies destroying them like a tsunami. Guard yourself from watching such "works" of filmdom and especially carefully guard your children. The higher bodies of children do not possess adequate protection yet and the whole nightmare they see on your TV screen simply programmes them on diseases and death.

We are warning you and trying to explain to you the reasons for your ailments.

At any moment you yourselves can break the vicious circle of the problems of your civilisation. The only thing required of you is just to make a decision and to act in your lives in harmony with the Divine principles.

And now I would like to touch upon one more important thing. Whenever you call to angels, God and the Masters to come to your help, always try to do it with humility of mind and to ask for help out of the point of piety both to the Life and the Creator.

This is because all mercy emanates from God, and it is only the impervious crust of egoism sticking all over your heart that prevents you from receiving this mercy.

I AM Hilarion, with Love towards you

An admonition for those on the Path

Lord Maitreya, January 9, 2007

I AM Maitreya, having come to you through my messenger!

I have come to forward a message about some urgent matters with which you ought to be familiarised.

You know that we come to you and that we have an opportunity to come due to the special dispensation. This dispensation allows us to communicate with you and give our messages through specially prepared individuals who serve us and hold posts of our messengers or bearers of news. And now we have a chance to speak through one of our messengers.

We are glad that the Teaching we give has received fairly wide publicity and that your hearts are opening to it. But, unfortunately, not all is as good as we expected it to be. And very many of you, after having found our Teaching given through our messenger, are set ablaze at the start, but after some time, retreat. The consciousness of such a person withers little by little and starts to be interested in the things that seduce him or her away from the right way – different trinkets of your world. You should learn to make a distinction between the true Teaching and the surrogates overabounding in your world.

We have already told you and I will repeat this one more time: ninety percent of the shelves in your bookshops groan with teachings that contain no more than ten percent of the Truth. And you make your choice in favour of these surrogates and turn away from the pleasures of our table kindly offered to you.

Why is it so? It is because in those numerous teachings that exist in your world one does not need to make a choice. One has neither to observe the discipline of a follower nor to have any obligations. Nothing is required of you, except for your energy, your Divine energy, which you use without control, giving your attention to surrogates. And the whole illusory world of pseudo-teachings exists only because you power it with your energy.

I will one more time repeat a guideline of the Teaching given to you earlier that you are responsible for every erg of the Divine energy you spend. It seems to you that you do nothing out of the ordinary. You simply attend seminars or go through training that seems useful for you. You spend your money, but - what is worst of all - you spend the Divine energy granted to you by God. You make your choice, and this choice makes you create karma.

Yes, beloved, you create karma by supporting false teachings. The point is that you are at different stages of development. And some of you are so innocent that you take for precious gems those imitations kindly offered to you that glitter on the surface but have no internal value.

But those of you who had an opportunity to taste the Truth, who read our Teachings and then suddenly felt a need to look for something else somewhere else, they bear the karma of the wrong choice and of the misuse of the Divine energy. And, as a rule, in this case you are guided by your ego. You feel dissatisfaction only because you do not want to part with that part of you which tells you: “There are many paths. It is not worth locking into only one thing. All the paths lead to God.”

However, this is a common mistake of your days, because there are paths that lead to God and there are paths that draw away from God.

I will give you a reliable guideline as to how not to err from your Path.

You should realise what it is that drives when you wish to seek some new fashionable teaching. What is your motive? As a rule, your ego whispers to you that you should not focus on only one thing and that there is nothing new in the dictations given by the Masters through their messenger.

And sure enough, there is really nothing new in our messages. We have been giving this Teaching through many of our messengers during many thousands of years. And if you had mastered at least ten percent of this Teaching, you would never barter this Teaching away for the baubles offered to you under the guise of our teachings.

Look for the reason for your leaving the Path inside of you. Only you yourselves make decisions and make choices. Unfortunately, we cannot make you follow the Path shown by us. You have freedom of choice, and you have a right to be guided with your free will while making choices in the physical plane.

However, your chances to make choices are given a timeframe. If you learn nothing and if from embodiment to embodiment you keep going under the thumb of your ego instead of parting with it, you receive a stern warning about your wrong choice. But if you stick to your guns and go on following your own path taking the bit between your teeth and closing your eyes, you are left alone.

Then only the actions of your intercessors in the Heavens, with whom you spend not just one embodiment together, can help you. But more often you are simply left alone, and you have to vegetate in the illusion during many embodiments until evolution gives your life-stream up as hopeless and you are recognised as needless ballast. God gets rid of the dead and ill cells. If a healthy body does not free itself from malignant cells which think only about themselves, the whole organism can fall ill.

That is why we come to you and with indefatigable pertinacity warn you over and over to think out all the steps you make in life.

Those people who have never heard of our Teaching and have never attended our classrooms bear one burden of a wrong choice of the path.

But those who have once decided to consecrate their embodiments to the service to the Brotherhood and have not applied the undertakings, are considered to be traitors and their karma is much greater than the karma of criminals and assassinators.

I have come with this message today. Perhaps, I have put some of you out of humour. But I had to give you this chance to think everything out and, after having conquered your ego, to make a considered decision posited on the standpoint of the Divine reason in you.

I will be glad to give a helping hand to those of you who ask for my help and who appeal to me at the minute of heavy contemplations over your destiny.

I AM Maitreya

Messages of Ascended Masters

The Masters about Karma

Tatyana N. Mickushina

Translated from Russian by
Svetlana Nekrasova

Proofreader: **Alison Lobel**

Websites:
http://sirius-eng.net (English version)
http://sirius-ru.net (Russian version)

39136651R00100

Made in the USA
San Bernardino, CA
20 September 2016